WATERCOLOURS OF SUSSEX PAST

by Mick Bensley
Verse by Bob Copper

BEN GUNN
1998

By the same author:
Watercolours of Norfolk Past

For Aimee, Russell
and Annie

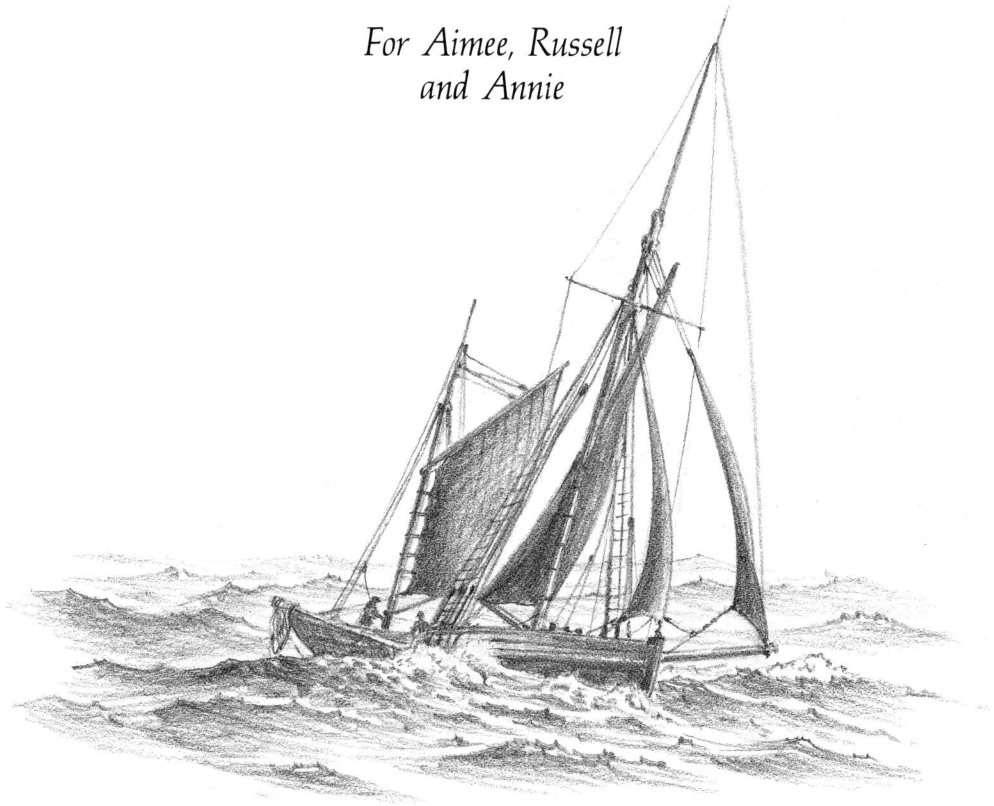

First published in 1998 by BEN GUNN

Design and typography by Mick Bensley

ISBN 0-9533998-0-X

Typeset in Palatino and
printed in England by Hartington Fine Arts Ltd., Lancing, Sussex

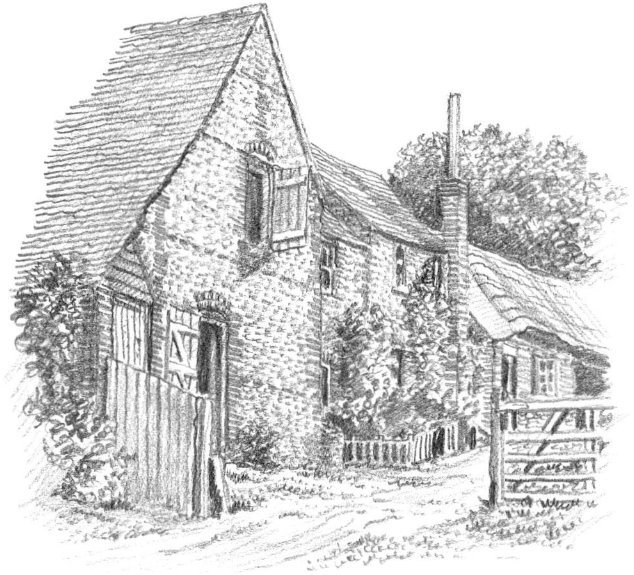

CONTENTS

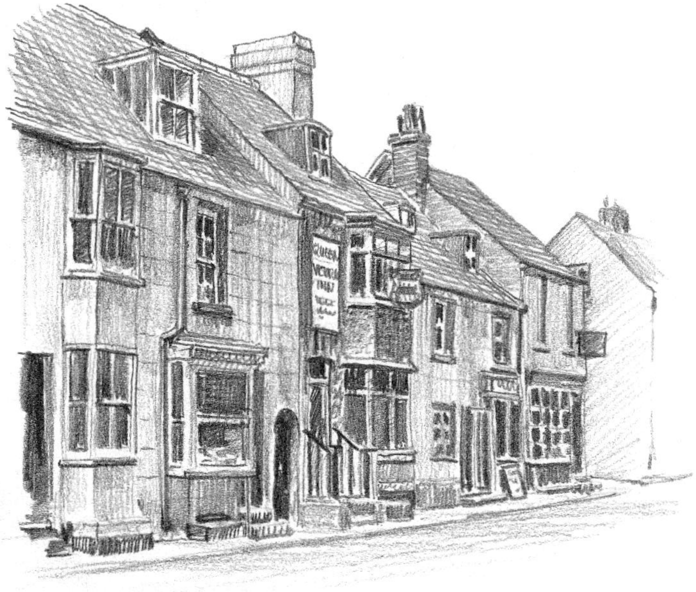

CONTENTS

INTRODUCTION

It is only in the last hundred years or so that the world we live in has changed so drastically. Up until about the turn of the century much of day to day life, particularly in the country, proceeded at the same pace as it had since the beginning of the millenium. The speed of transport and the amount of work completed in a day was governed to a great extent by the pace set by the lumbering beasts of burden with whom life on the farm was so closely linked. A ploughman with his team of horses or oxen was expected to plough one acre of land a day the same as his Saxon counterpart, and the Elizabethan shepherd would have been quite at home tending his flock on the Sussex Downs with his dog and crook and relieving them of their heavy fleeces in summer with hand-shears. This peaceful, plodding tenor of life was reflected also in the speed of thought and speech and life was altogether a more leisurely and less frenetic affair.

We cannot travel back in time but it is at least fascinating and perhaps salutory to cast an eye over our shoulders from time to time to see what we have discarded at the road-side on our path to progress.

In this book Mick Bensley has, with his undoubted artistic skills and keen perception, recreated scenes of Sussex life, many set in locations familiar to us, as they must have been in those distant, more measured but admittedly more arduous times. We see that world not in a pipe-dream of romanticism but with a down-to-earth and "tell it like it was" reality. Mick's particular skills lie not merely in portraying the scene but in capturing the atmosphere and the ambient mood of the moment.

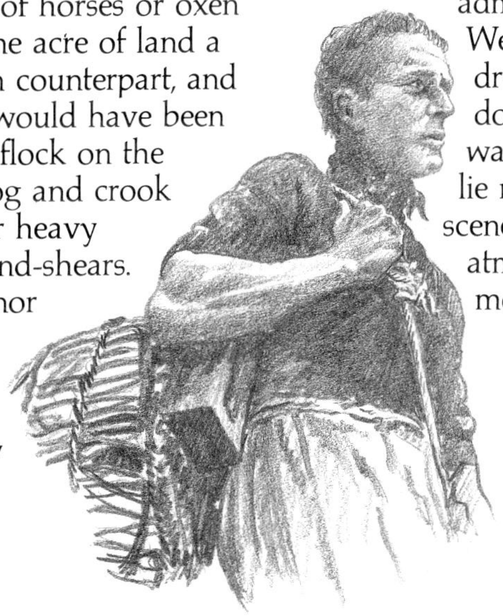

MICK BENSLEY was born in Sheringham on the North Norfolk coast. He trained at the Norwich School of Art and then moved to London where he worked as a graphic designer and illustrator for the next fifteen years.

In his spare time he developed his painting skills and in 1980, moved back to his native Norfolk where he took up painting full-time.

His marine and landscape paintings from this period were widely exhibited and are in private collections worldwide. Some of the most popular are reproduced in his first book "Watercolours of Norfolk Past".

Growing up in a coastal town gave Mick a love of the sea. He is internationally known for his Lifeboat rescue scenes. In 1988, a major exhibition was held of forty-four paintings reconstructing rescues from around the British coast line. This was the result of three and a half years work which involved researching each service carefully from the R.N.L.I. records.

In 1989 Mick moved to Rottingdean alternating his work as an illustrator/designer and painting his beloved marine and landscapes.

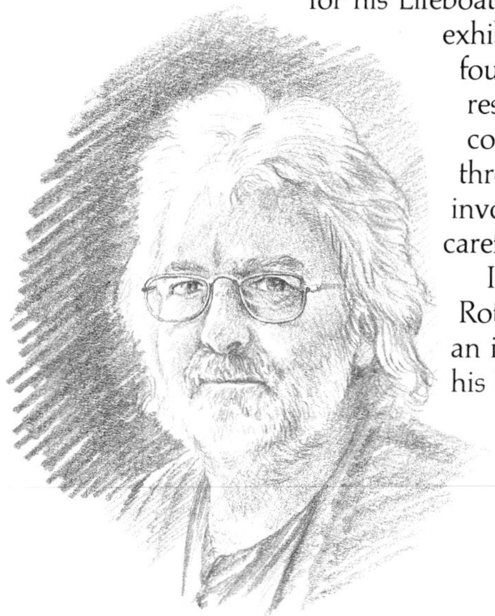

BOB COPPER was born in Rottingdean in 1915 and attended the village school there, leaving in 1929 to become a lather-boy in the village barber's shop. Later he enlisted in the Life Guards and in 1936 joined what was then the West Sussex Constabulary.

After ten years in the police force, he took over a social club in Peacehaven. He is now retired, having handed the running of the club over to his son John, with whom, together with his daughter Jill and son-in-law Jon Dudley, he keeps alive the family singing tradition. They appear regularly at folk festivals and concerts in this country and the USA and make television and radio programmes.

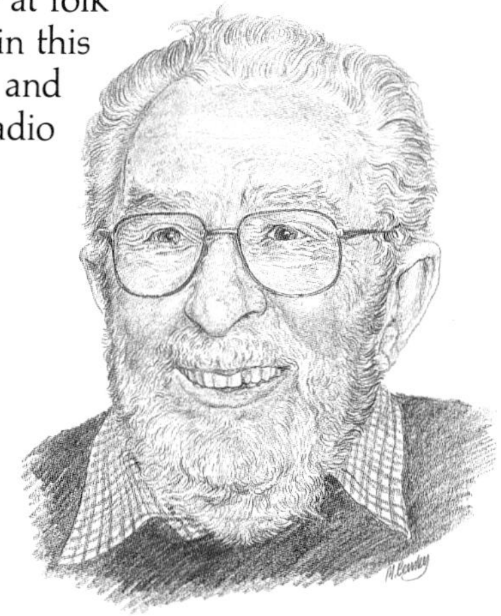

the
PLATES

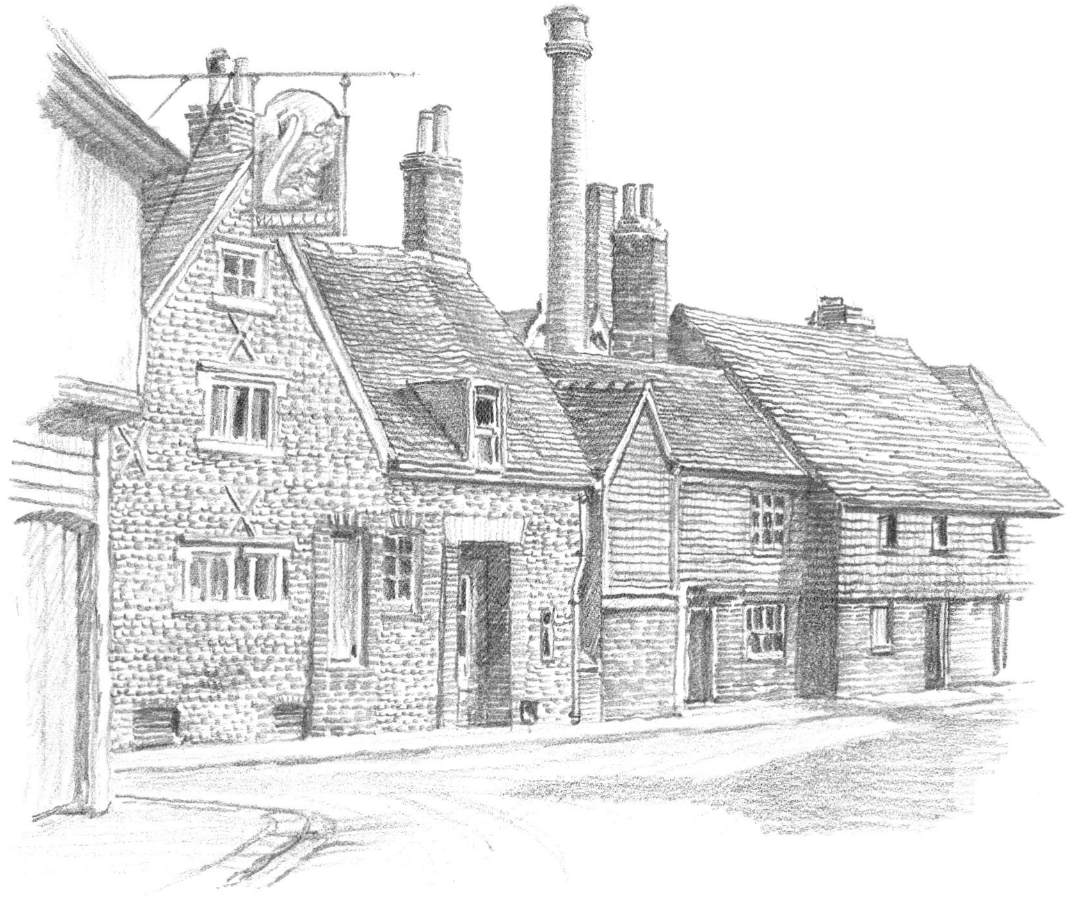

Rye, Winter Sun

Watercolour 10 x 16 ins 1994

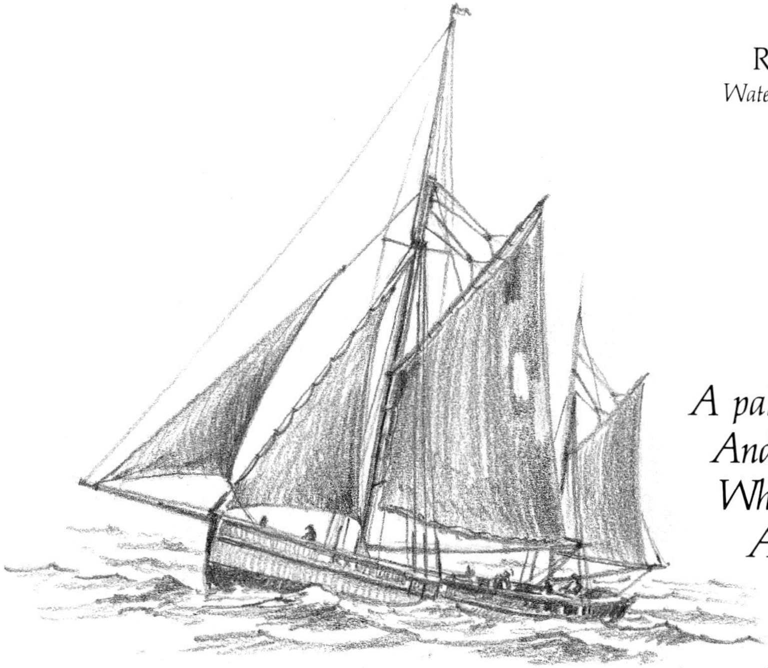

A pallid sun struggles fitfully through
And lights a wintry scene,
Where men pit their strength and skills
Against the elements to wrest
A living from the sea;
Like the gulls that wheel and scream
Around their heads so hungrily,
And than whom they fare only slightly better.

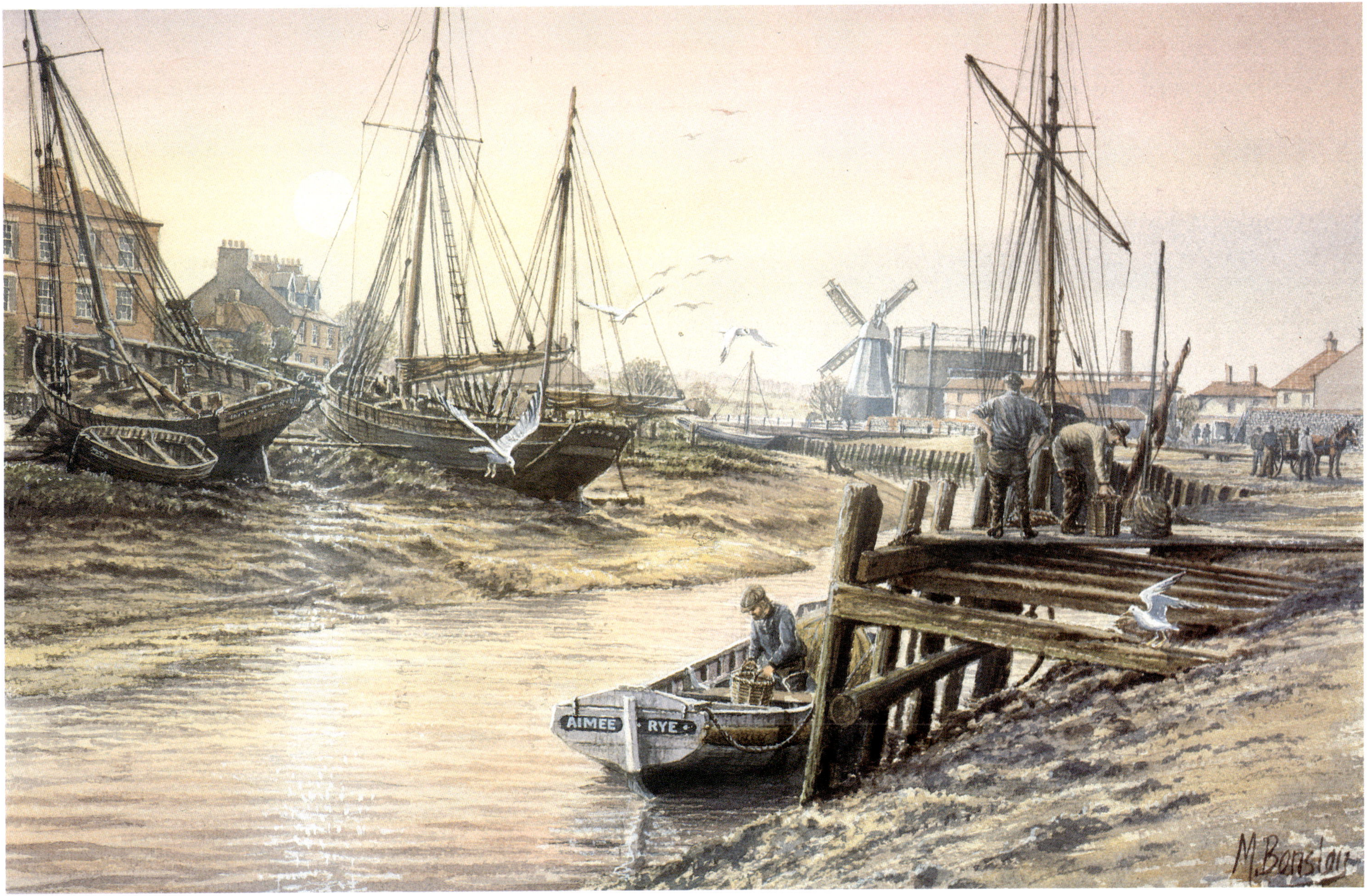
AIMEE
RYE
M.Bonslow

Rottingdean High Street, Late Spring

Watercolour 9½ x 15 ins 1998

The golden light of afternoon
Shines down through beech and sycamore;
The street winds gently 'twixt stout walls
Of boulders from the nearby shore.
And folk on foot need fear no car
When strolling, in all probability,
To catch or miss the evening post
In an age of deep tranquility.

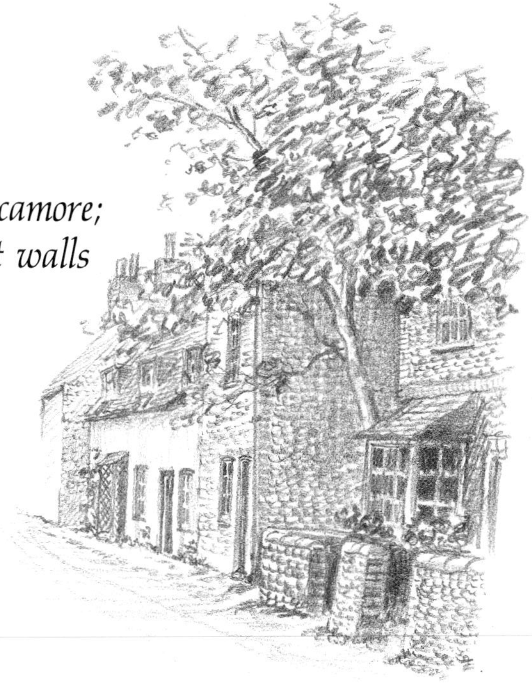

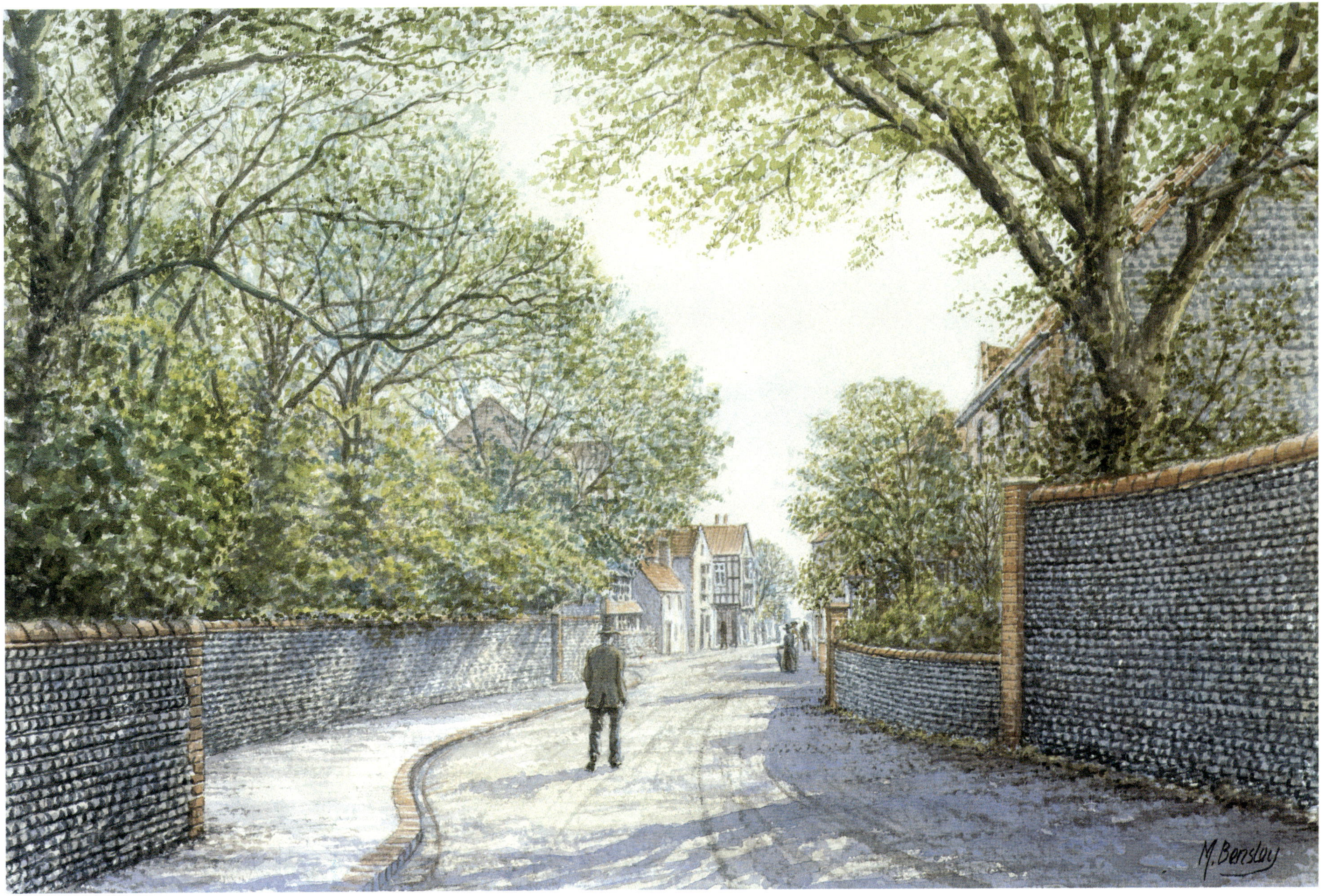
M. Bensley

Newhaven Lifeboat 'Sir Fitzroy Clayton'
on call to the Danish schooner
'Morgens Koch', Dec. 1929
Watercolour 11 x 21 ins 1994

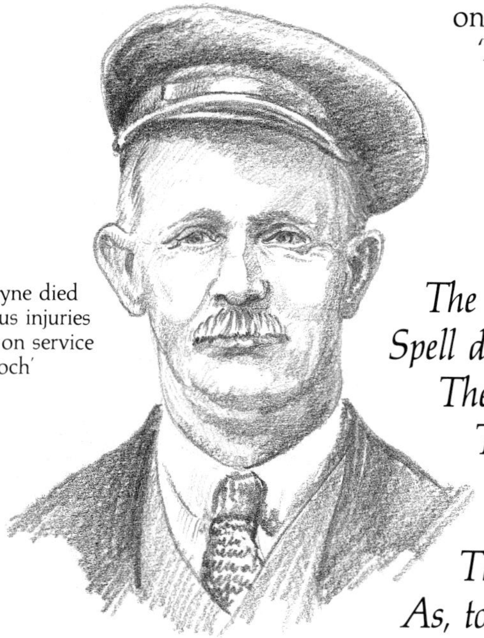

Coxswain Dick Payne died as a result of serious injuries he received whilst on service to the 'Morgens Koch'

The rising seas and low'ring clouds
Spell danger to this stricken crew.
The tempest screaming in the shrouds
They muster aft and
Pray as only sailors do.

The helpless watch the helpful's skill
As, to a man and with a will,
They strive like mariners of old
And use the strength of tide and wind
To resolve the very situation
These forces have created.

The lifeboat slowly closes in
Driven by wind and borne by tide,
But by the sea-anchor controlled,
Until at last she lays 'longside.
The storm still unabated.

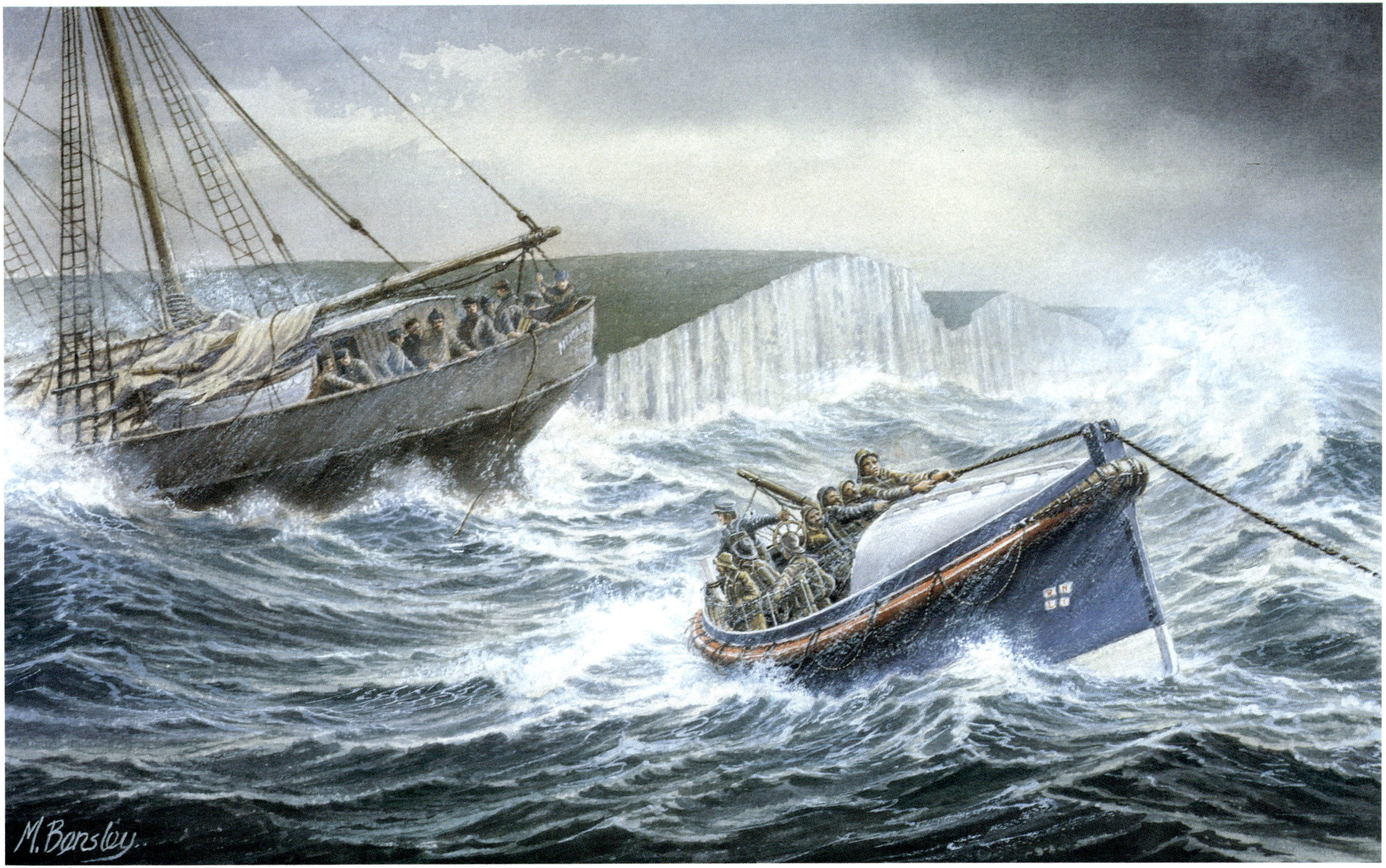
M. Bensley

Ovingdean Church

Watercolour 10 x 16 ins 1998

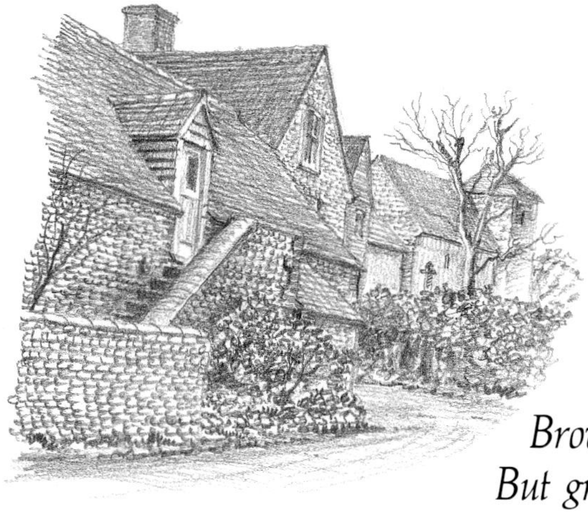

Brown leaves mark the waning year,
But grass is green though leaves are sere.
Flowers for the dead while kinfolk mourn,
But courtship lives and the world's reborn.

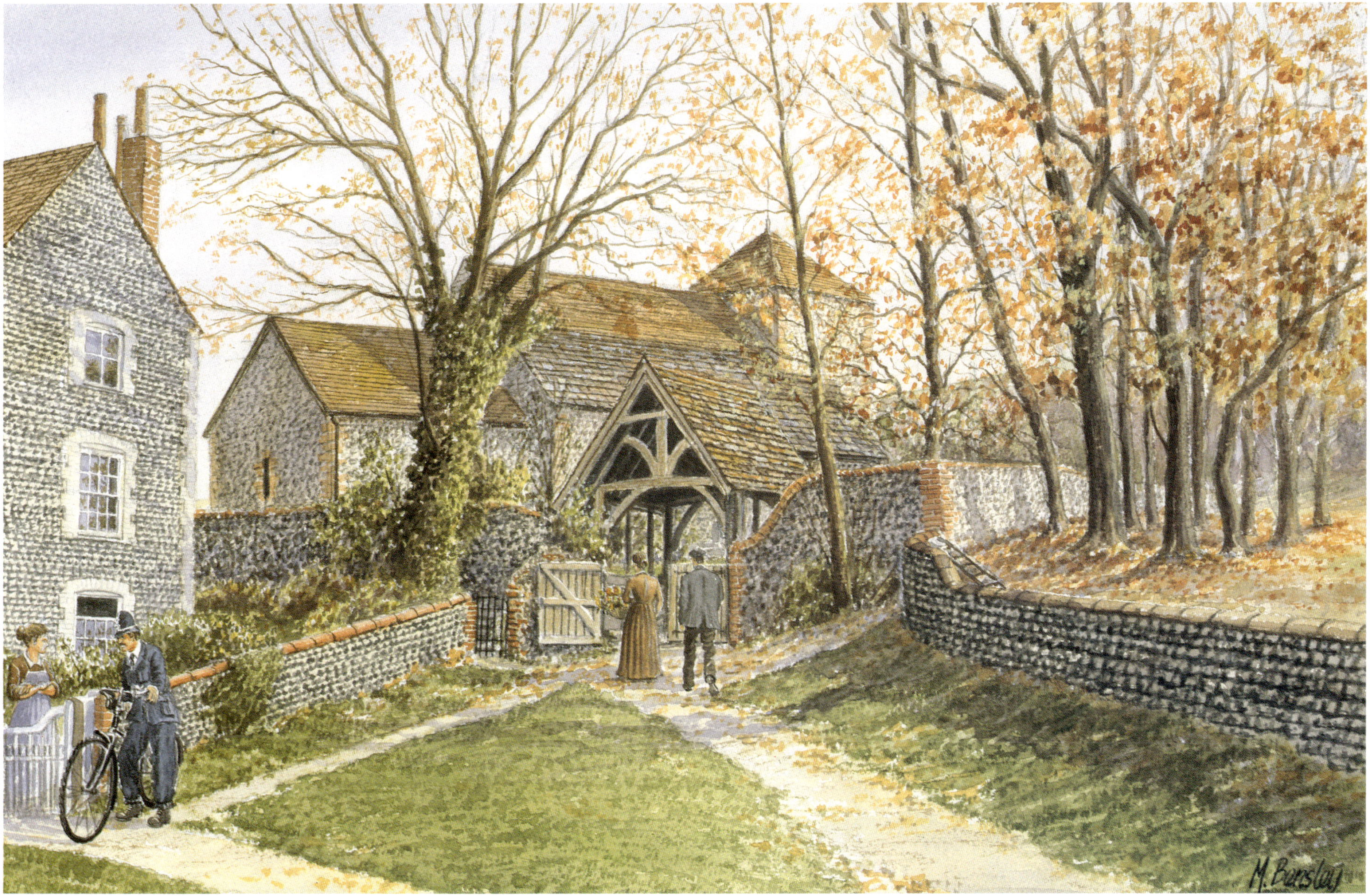
M. Bursley

Rottingdean beach

Watercolour 10 x 15 ins 1998

Since time out of mind the rough seas of the Channel
Have eroded and eaten the crumbling chalk cliffs,
And men's breakwaters and groynes
Have slowed but not halted
The tidal advance which just cast them adrift.

Three generations of coastal construction,
All shown in their various states of repair,
Illustrate how they're destined to fall to destruction;
Today not a sign of e'en one of them's there.

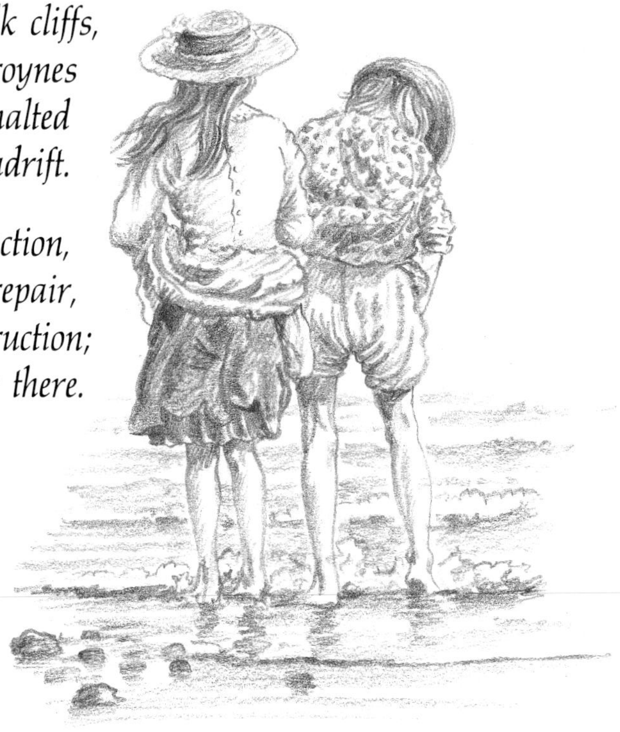

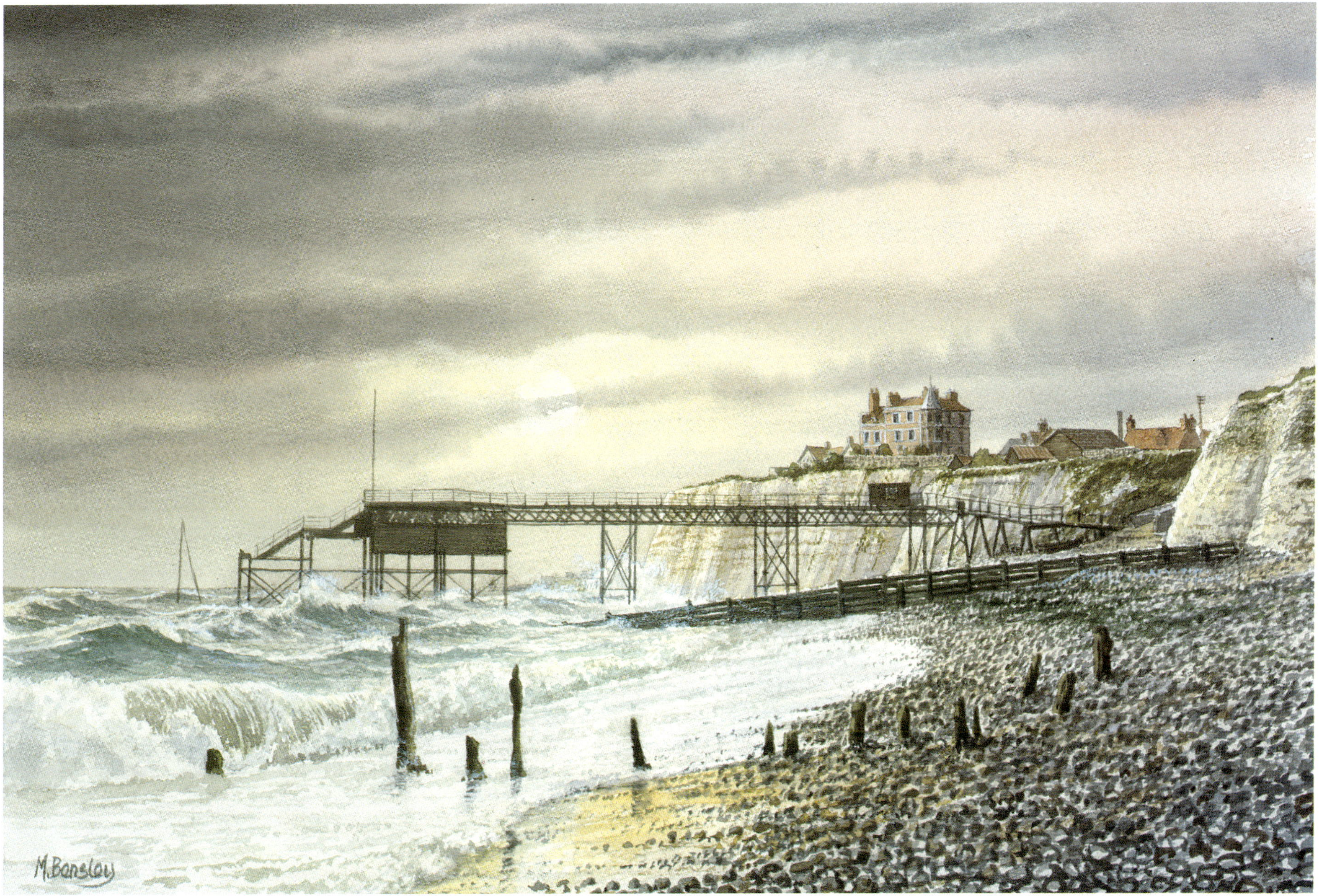
M.Bensley

Steyning, early start
Watercolour 10 x 16 ins 1997

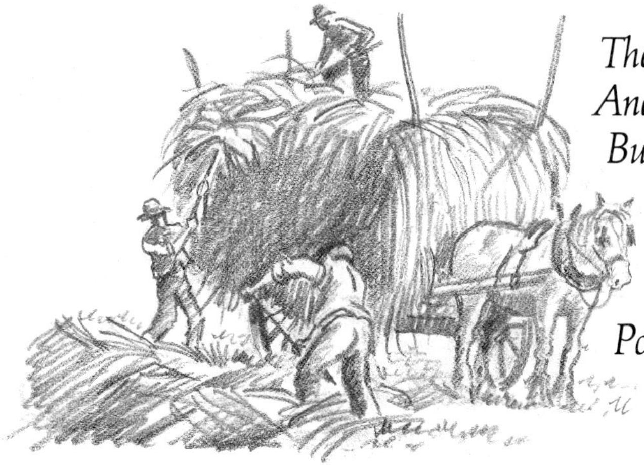

The empty street echoes to the sound of hoofs
And the rumble and crunch of iron-shod wheels.
But Morpheus reigns supreme
Beneath these ancient roofs;
The curtains drawn,
The blackbird's song of morn
Pours forth unheard, and still they dream,
But farmwork must proceed.

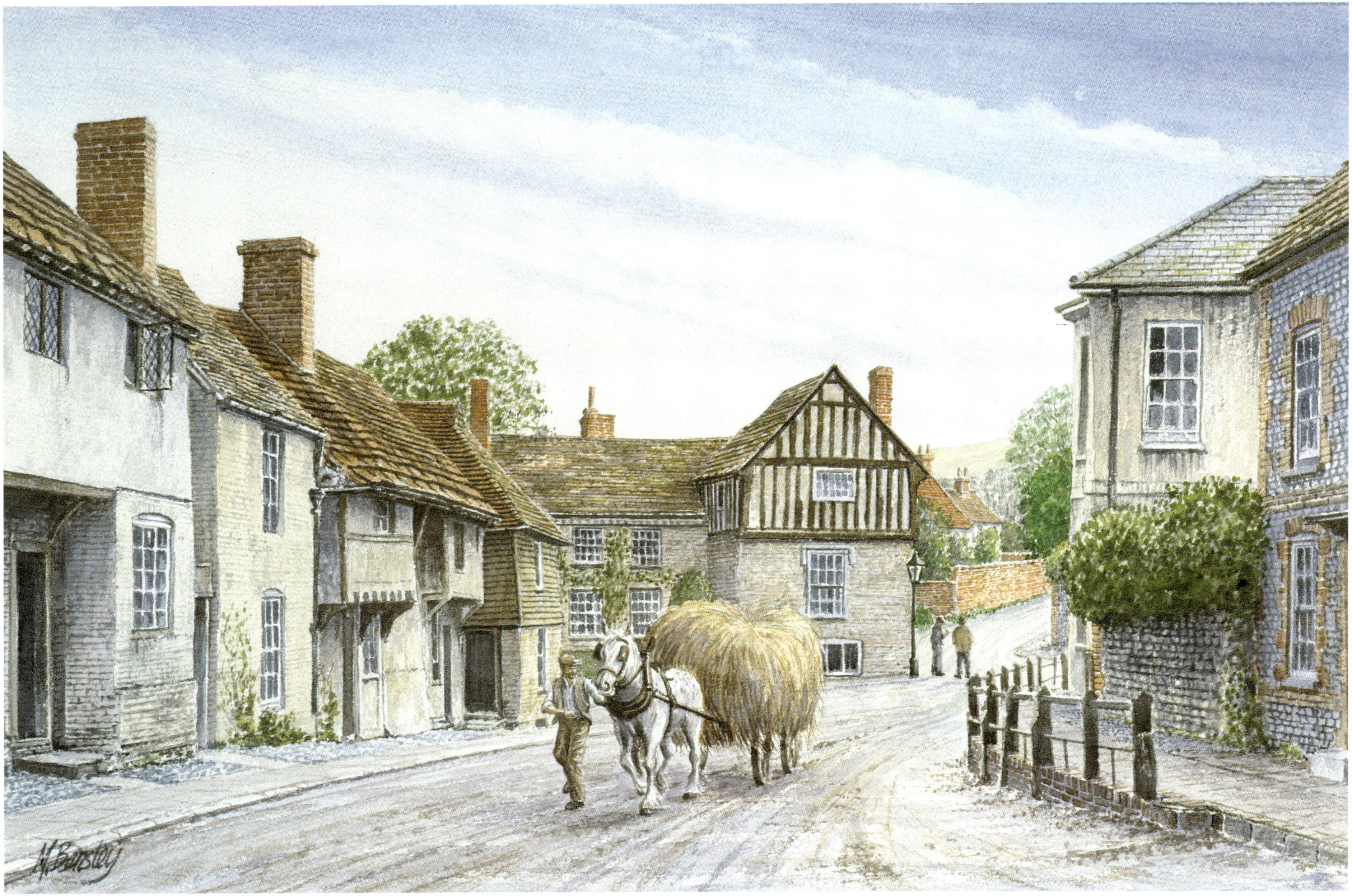

Arundel, February afternoon

Watercolour 12 x 18 ins 1997

The day like the voyage draws close to its end.
With a following breeze and a fast flowing tide,
Their thoughts turn to home as they take the last bend,
The home-wharf once more to tie up a alongside.
The familiar sight of the town's classic frieze
Means they could be, with luck, home in time for their teas.

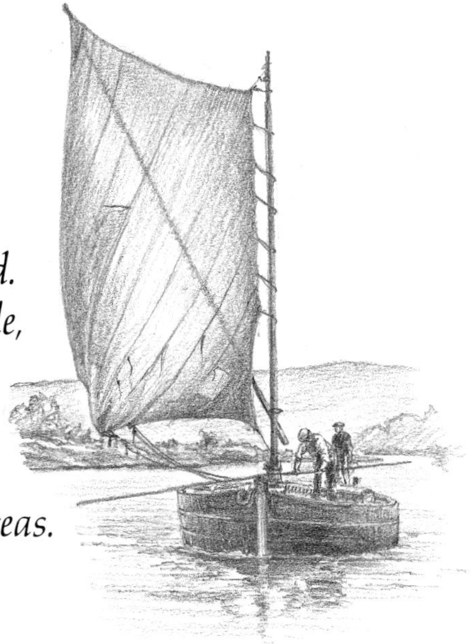

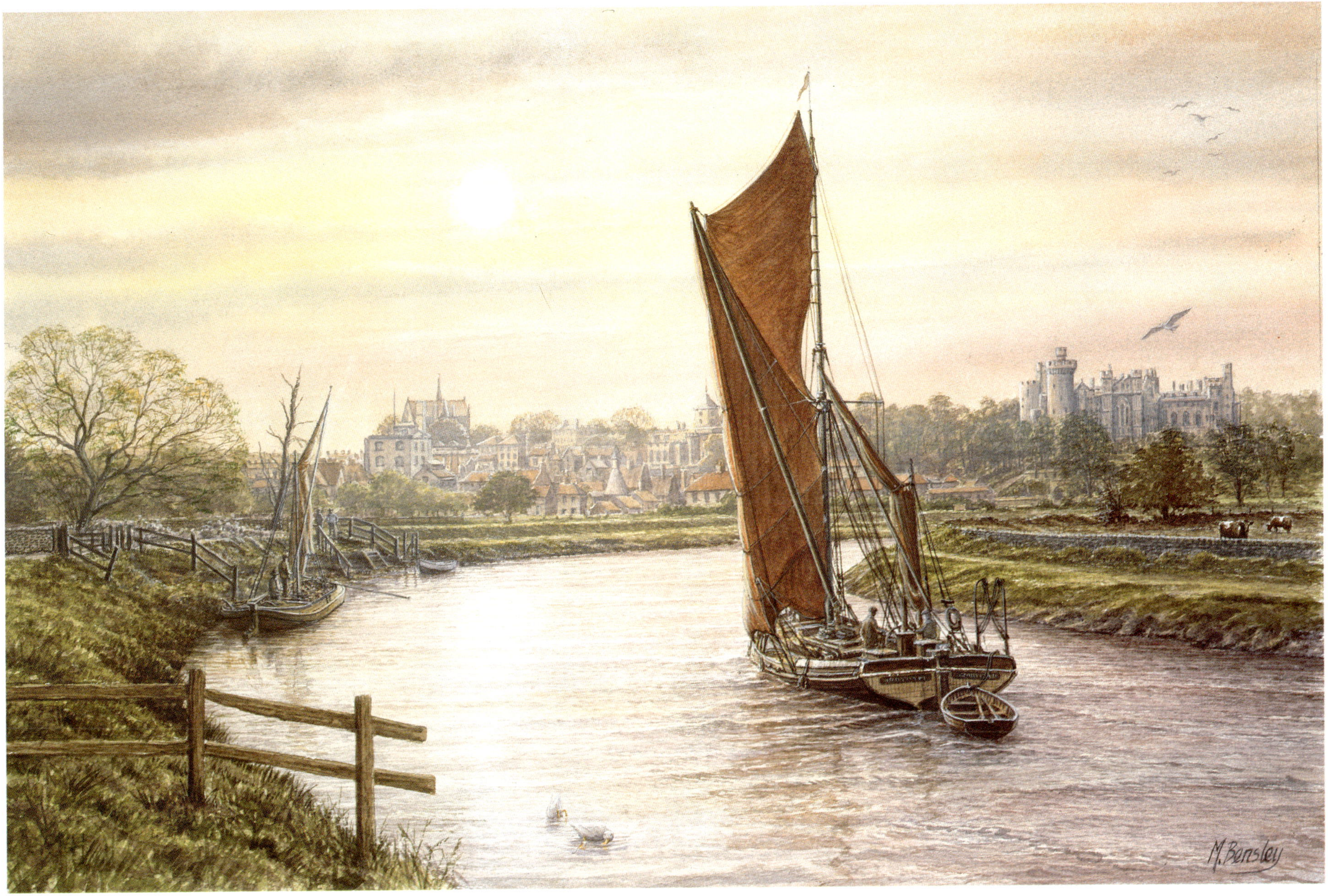
M. Bensley

The Italian cargo ship 'Nimbo' aground,
at Portobello, Telscombe Cliffs, Nov. 1929
Watercolour 17 x 28 ins 1998

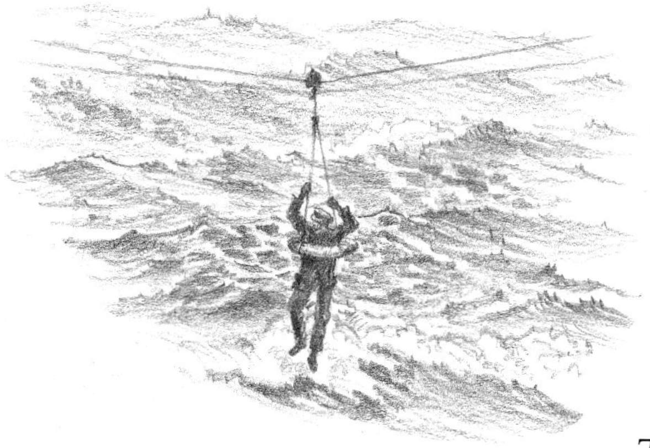

What an inglorious arrival and entry
Into England for the sunny-natured crew
Of this Italian cargoe-ship.
Driven hard ashore under the chalk cliffs
Of Sussex before a wild, November gale,
They were brought ashore one by one
By breeches-buoy
Swinging and plunging crazily
On long, looping ropes like inept trapeze acrobats,
At the mercy of wind and gravity,
They finally felt the the firm tread of cliff-top turf
Beneath their feet. Wet, cold and dejected
But safe on shore.

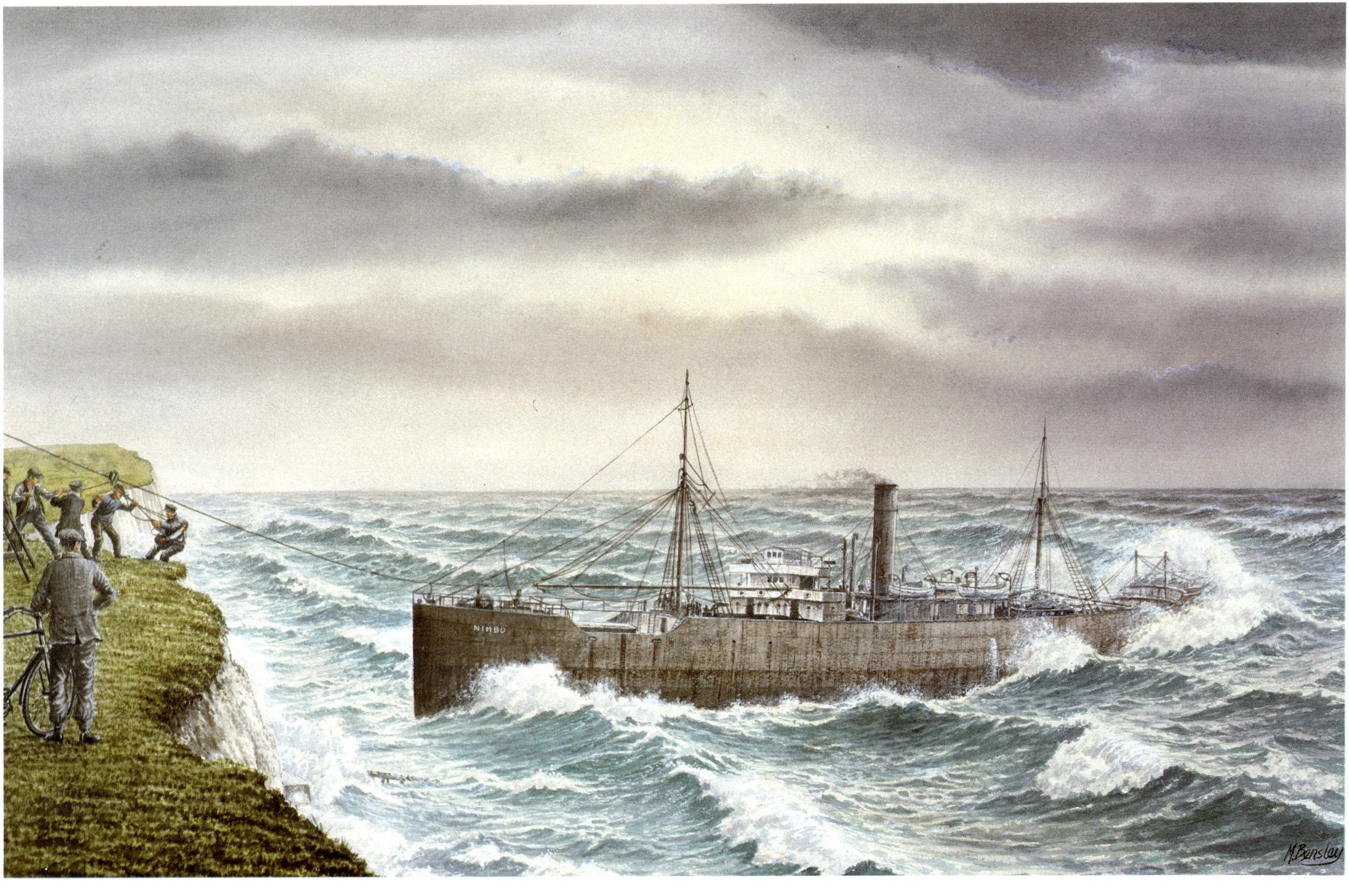
NIMBO
M.Bensley

The Village Forge, Rottingdean

Watercolour 9½ x 15 ins 1998

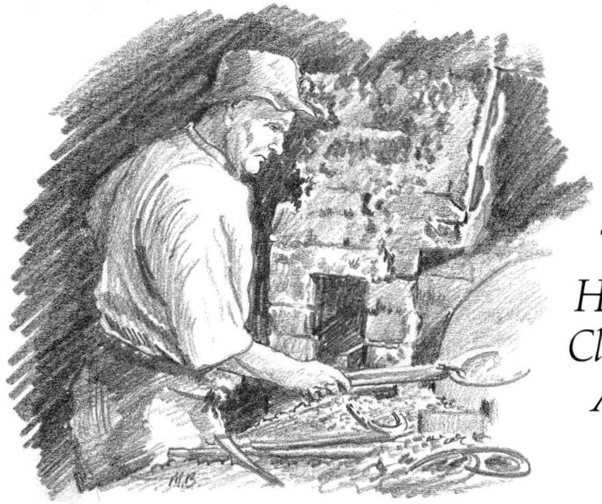

The village smithy bends his back
Swopping the while the chit and chat of local news.
His expert hands move deftly as he shoes
The patient mare.
His hammer blows make the anvil ring
Clear out across the morning air
And challenge the church-bell's call to prayer.

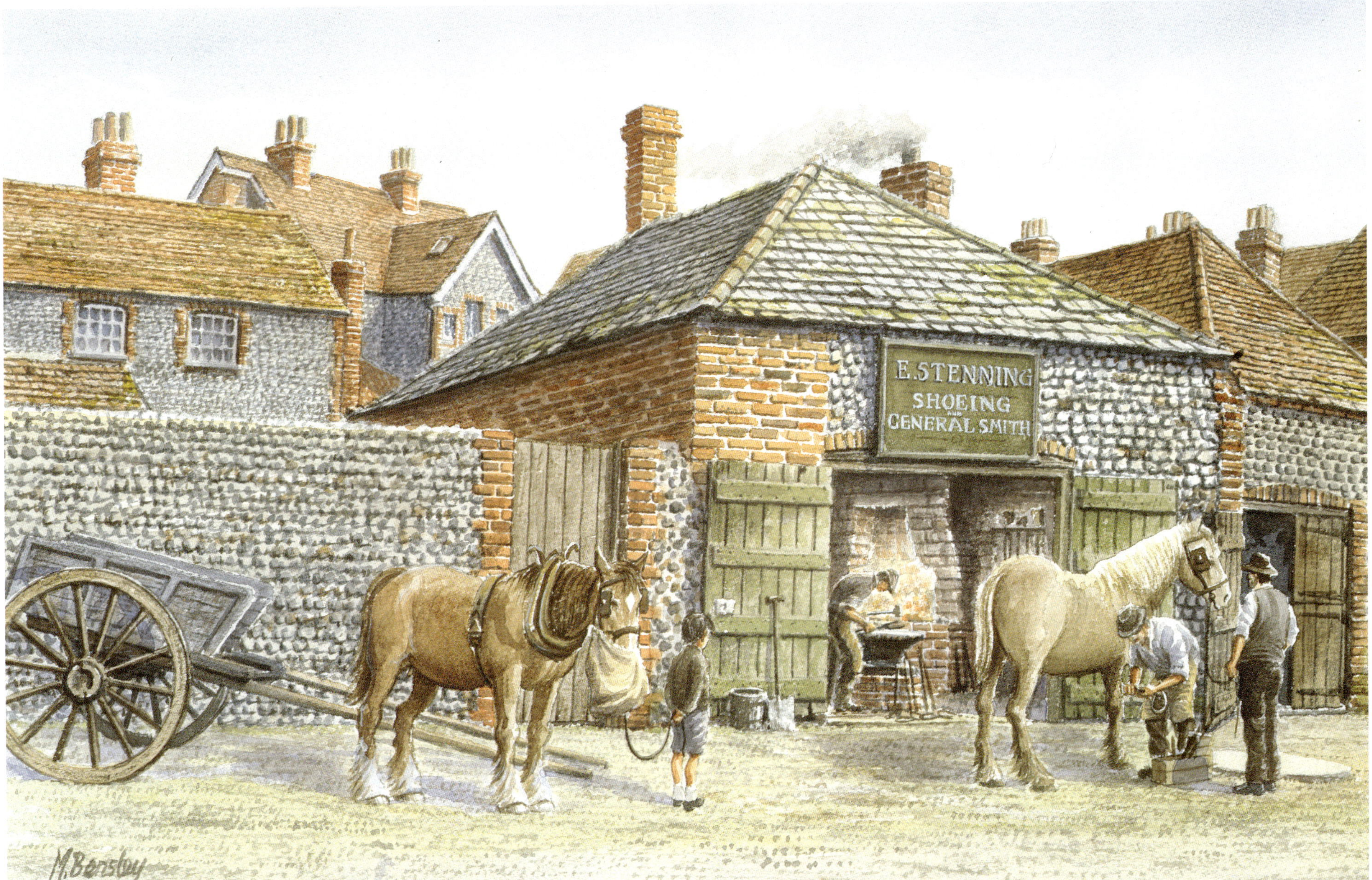
E. STENNING
SHOEING
AND
GENERAL SMITH
M. Bensley

Boat repairs, Piddinghoe
Watercolour 10 x 16 ins 1997

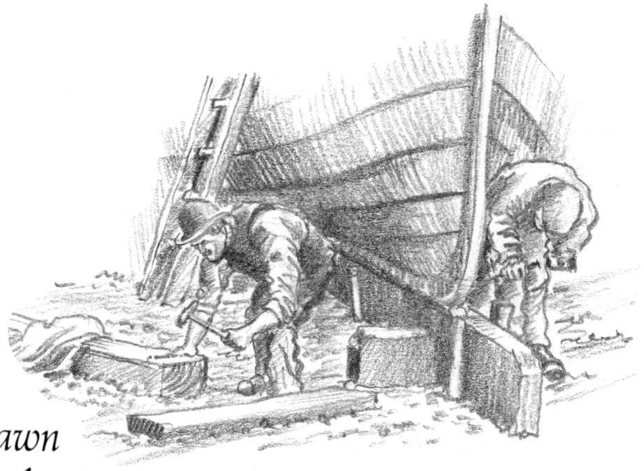

The working day returns in a pewter dawn
And with it comes the tide,
Nosing its way into every creek and inlet.
The sounds of hammer and timber sawn
Shatter the early silence and little boats
Asleep on the river bank are stirred into life
And bob and tug at their moorings to greet the morn.

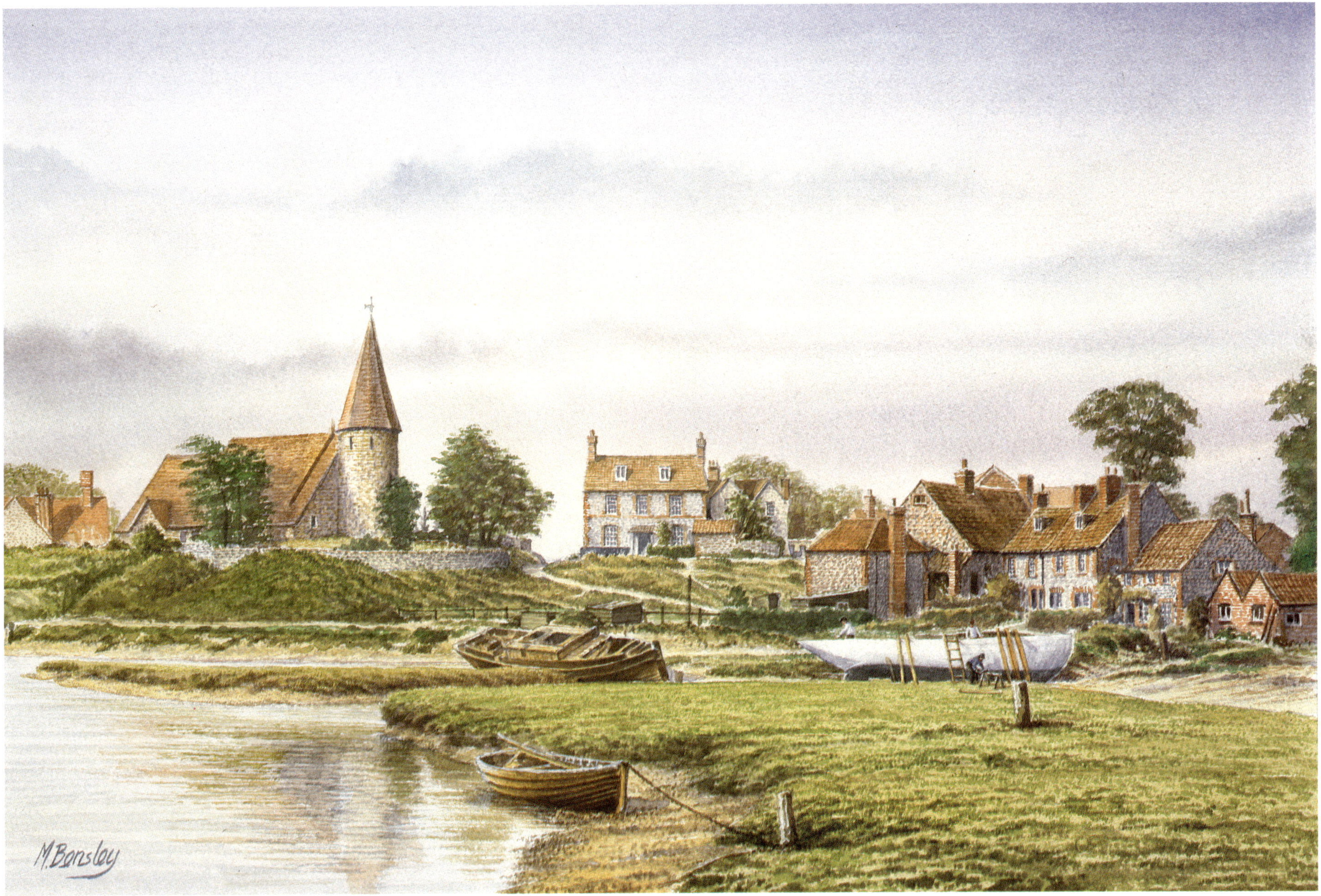
M.Bonsley

Hauling the pots off Saltdean cliffs
Watercolour 12 x 18 ins 1998

Due to constant erosion
On this part of the coast,
And the inland, tidal creep,
We were lifting our lobster pots
From the land on which
Our great-great-grandfathers
Dug bank and ditch,
And grazed their flocks of sheep.

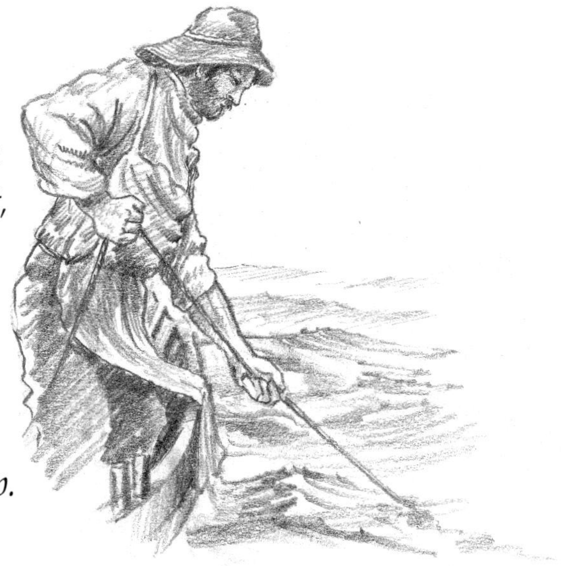

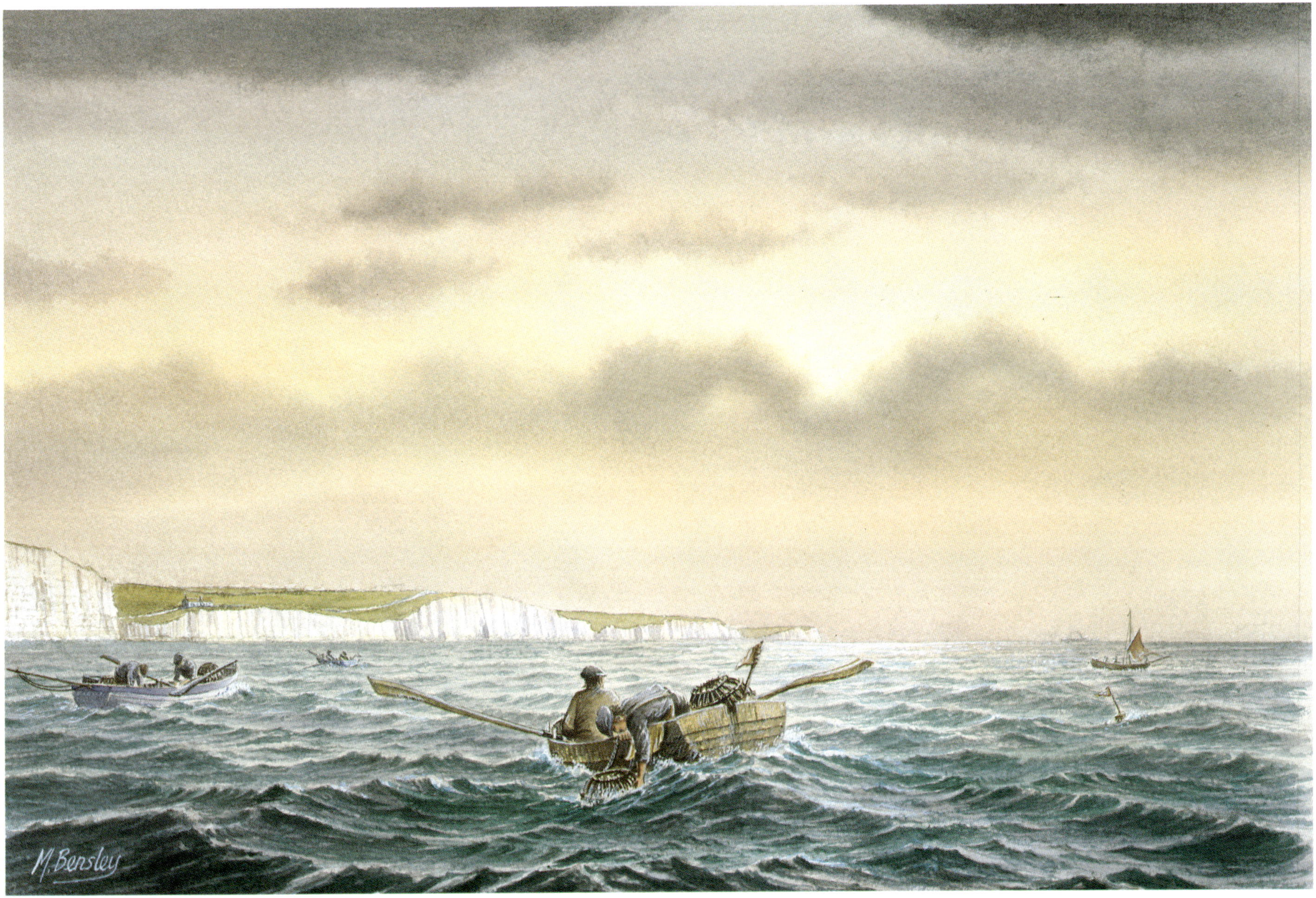
M.Bensley

Rottingdean Windmill
Watercolour 10 x 15 ins 1998

On Beacon Hill, where the fires were lit
To warn the nation of the Armada's approach,
And which saw, later, the serpentine vapour-trails
Of planes engaged in the Battle of Britain
Over the harvest fields of Southern England,
The lone, black windmill, with arms upraised,
Still stands to remind us of the long
And eventful history we possess.

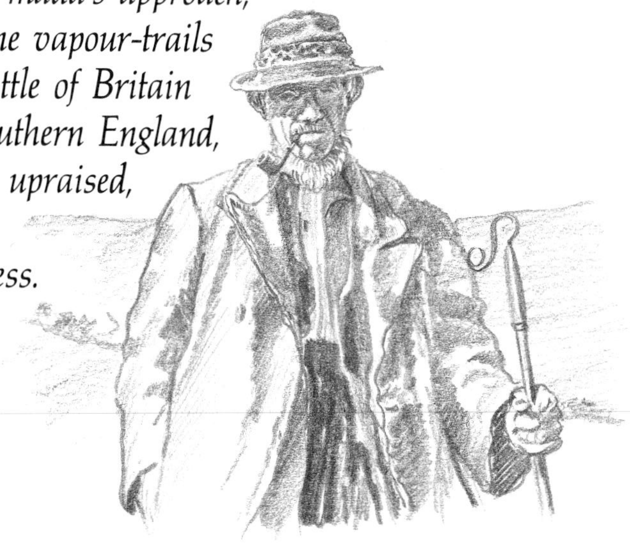

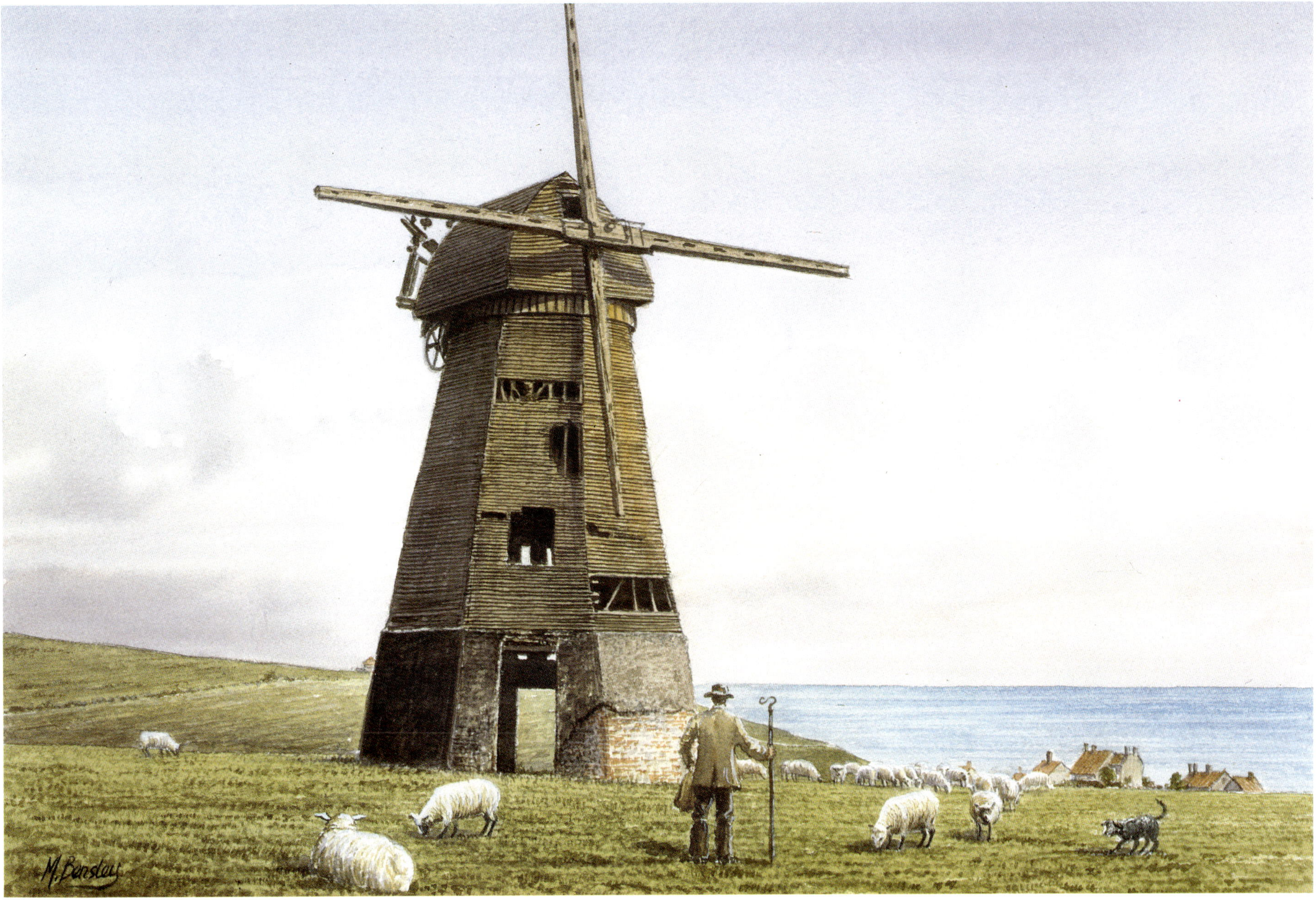
M. Bensley

Kingston

Watercolour $9\frac{1}{2}$ x 15 ins 1998

Just a man and a horse slowly
Clip-clopping up a village street,
Under the steep shoulder of a high chalk down,
As in the days of yore:
So, why should I feel sad?

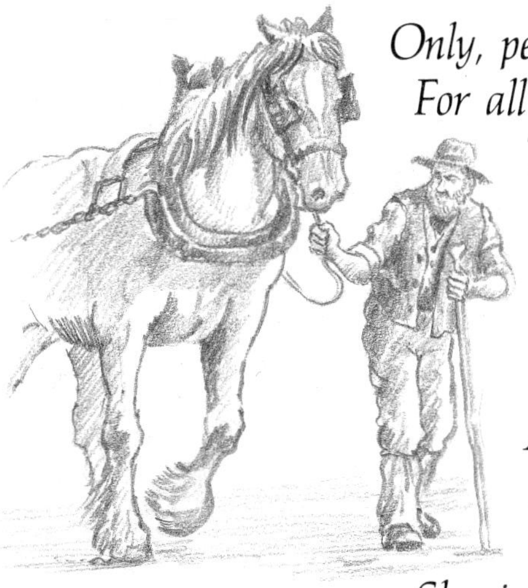

Only, perhaps, because he stands
For all those that went before.
The village folk who here,
Beneath these red-tiled, wrinkled roofs,
Where cottage hearths glowed warm
And well-springs ran cool and clear,
Saw a thousand golden harvest moons
And as many Magi's stars,
As on this soil they worked
And from this soil lived;
Sleeping, waking, working, playing,
Planning and praying
While their children thrived:

And we shall never see their like again.

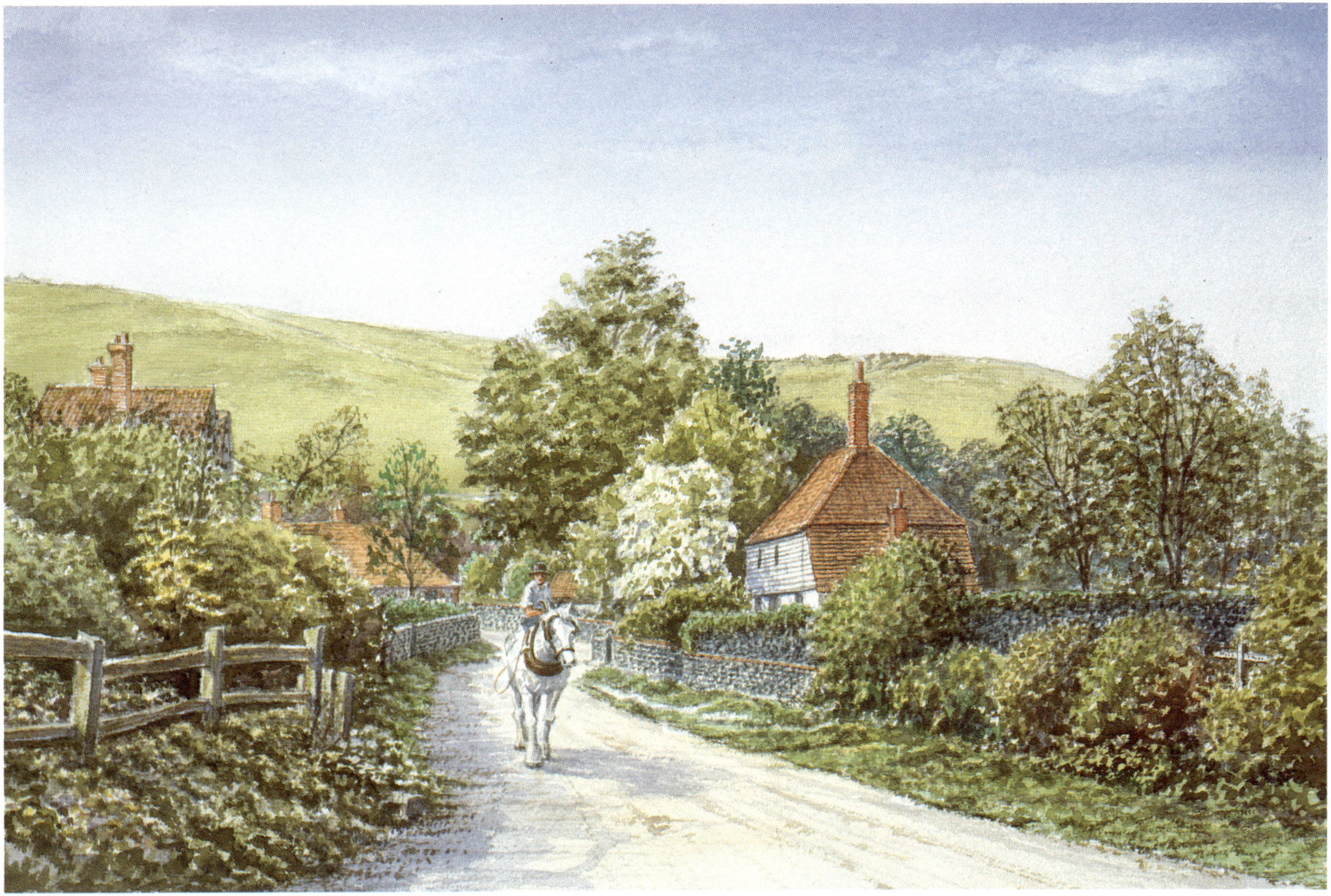

The Shoreham lifeboat 'William Restell' being towed
by the tug 'Stella' to the 'Anirac', Aug. 1912

Watercolour 12 x 20 ins 1987

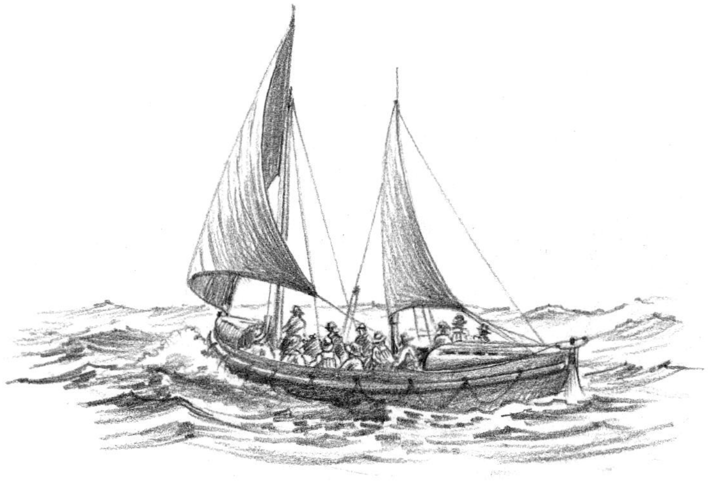

Luffing and yawing and "shipping 'em green",
Man-power yields to the forces of steam.
May the luck these men pray for when heaving the trawl
Be their's as they answer this desperate call.

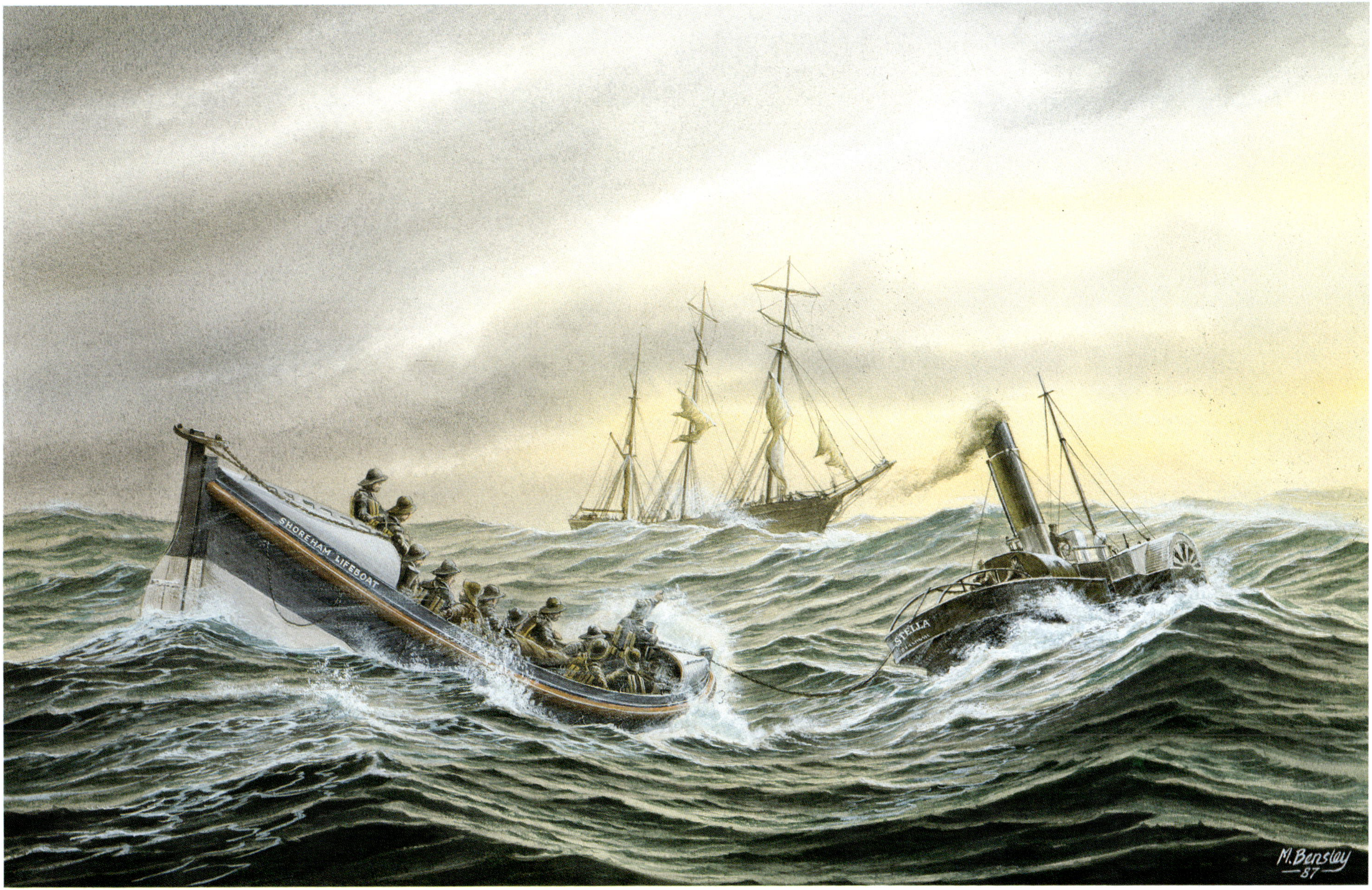
SHOREHAM LIFEBOAT
STELLA
M. Bensley
87

Ovingdean Grange Farmyard
Watercolour 10 x 16 ins 1998

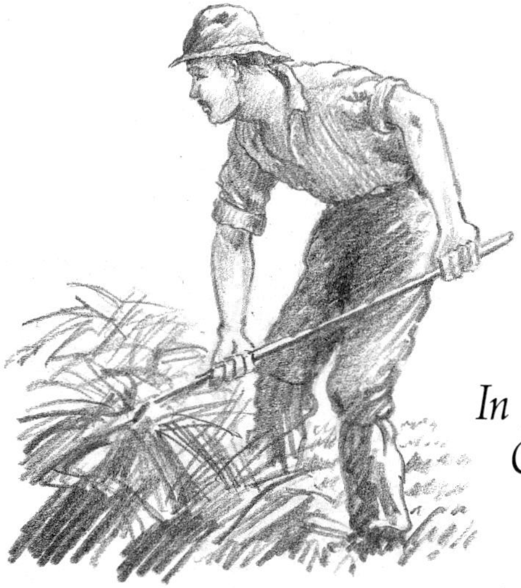

In from the heat of the hayfield
Comes the fragrant wainload
Into this quiet corner of the home farmyard,
Where fowls forage for fallen grain
And the team for a brief respite nuzzle their nosebags.
But men must work apace building the stack
For next winter's provender.

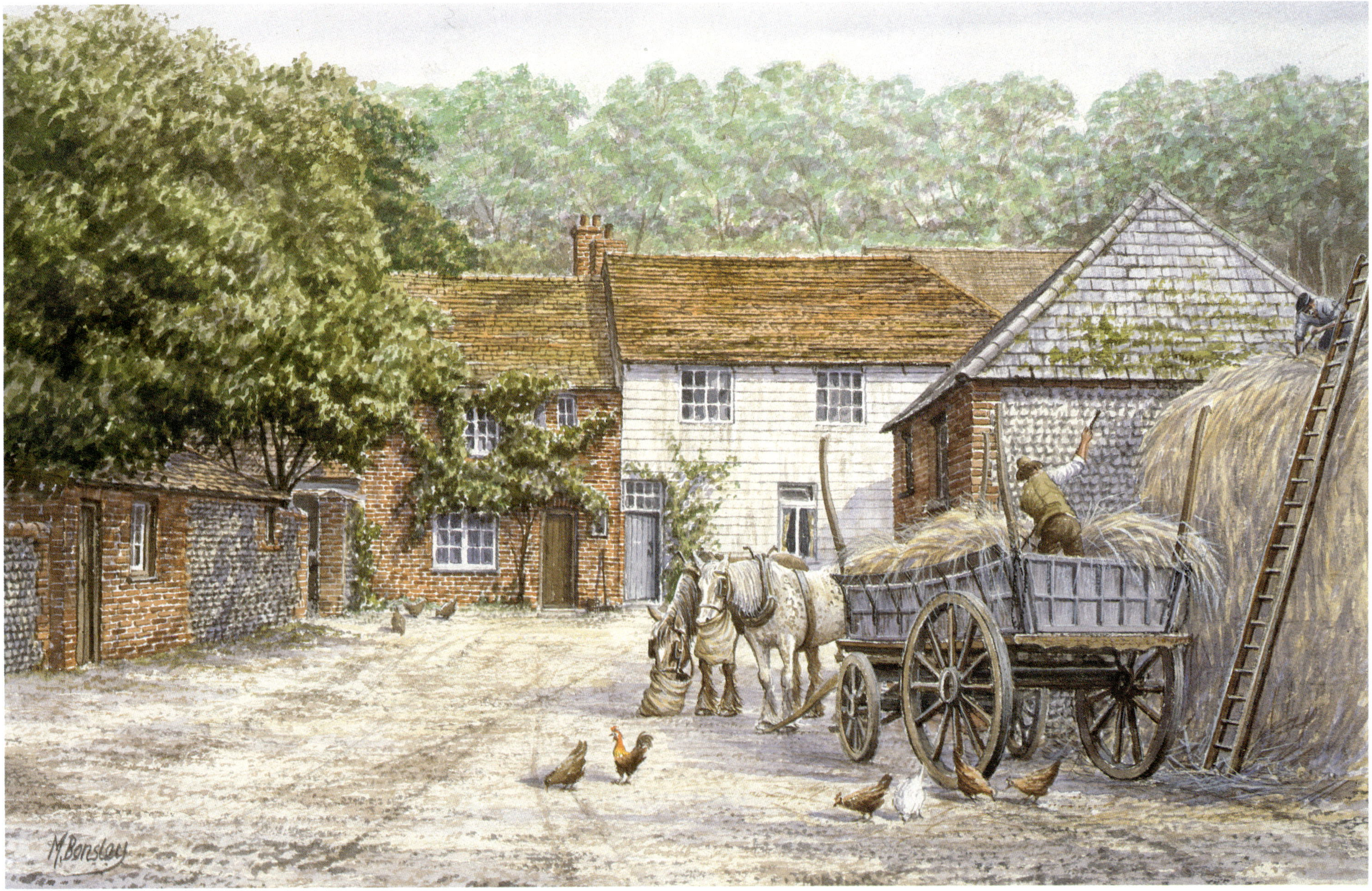
M. Bensley

Night Fleet heading for Brighton

Watercolour 14 x 36½ ins 1997

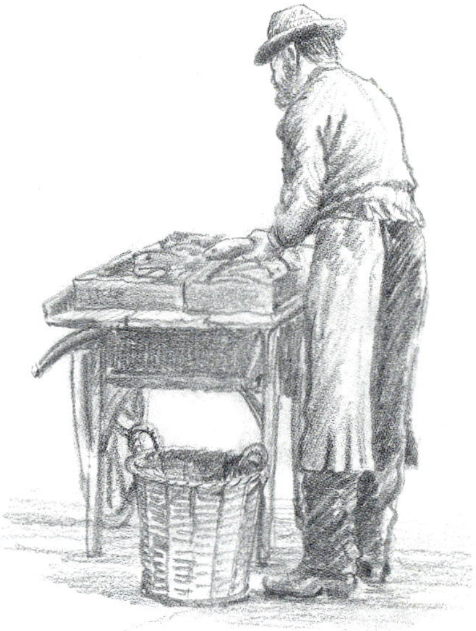

First in, highest prices.
(The early bird the fat worm snatches)
The all-night fleet strain boom and yard,
Resorting to all the tricks and devices
At their disposal to get their catches
Into the market on Brighton Hard.

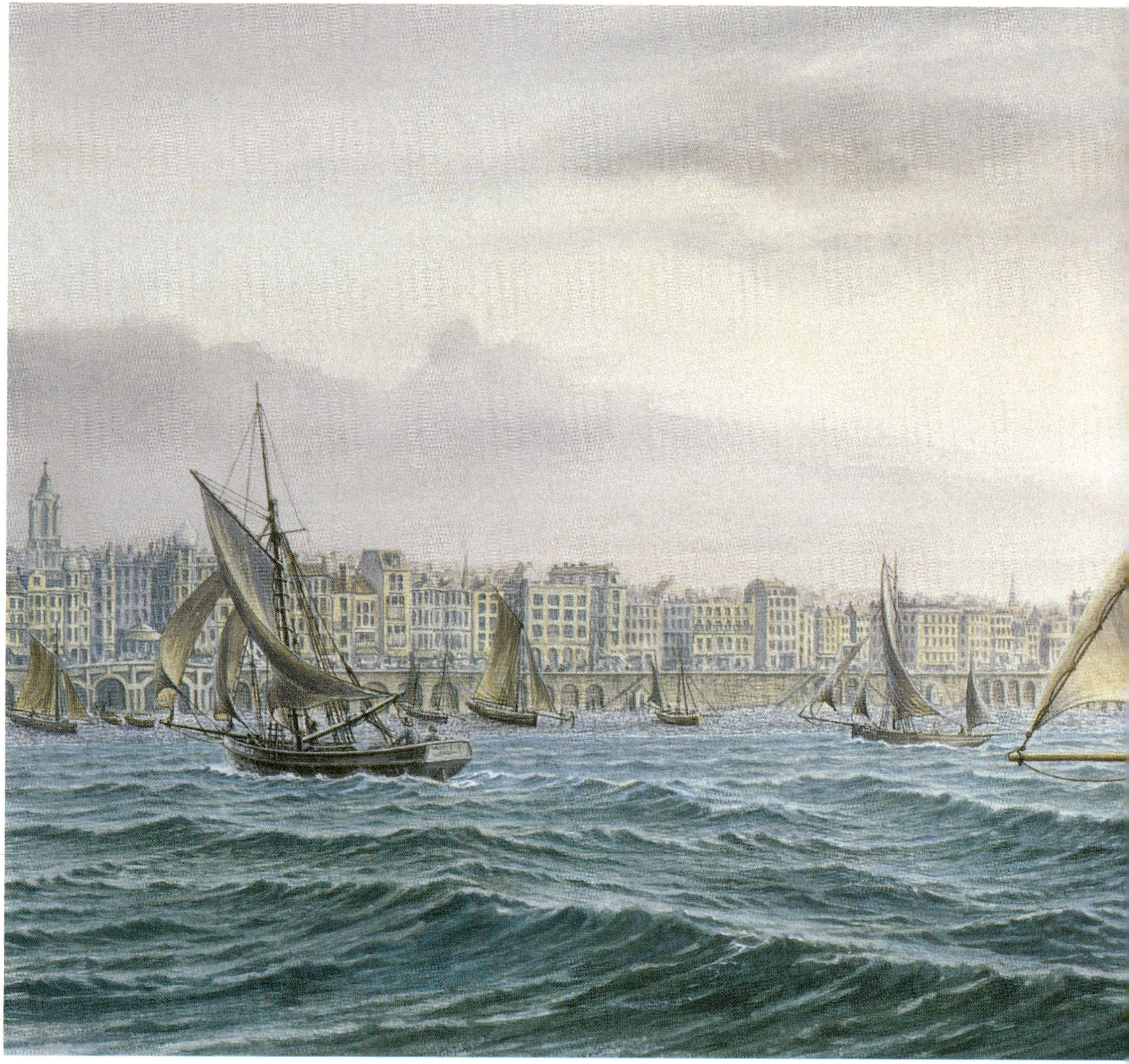

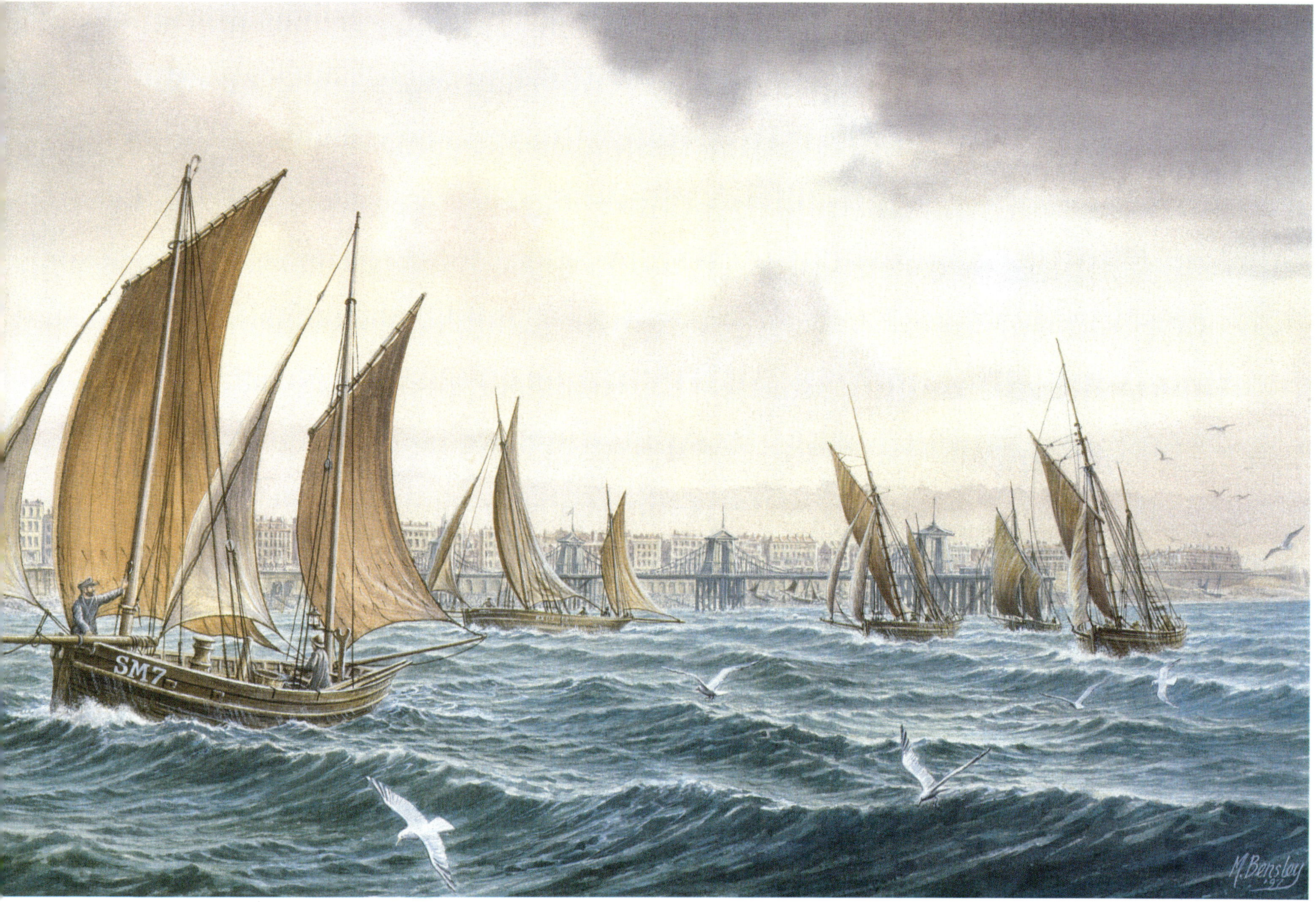
SM7
M. Bensley '97

View from the Downs Road, Woodingdean
Watercolour 10 x 16 ins 1998

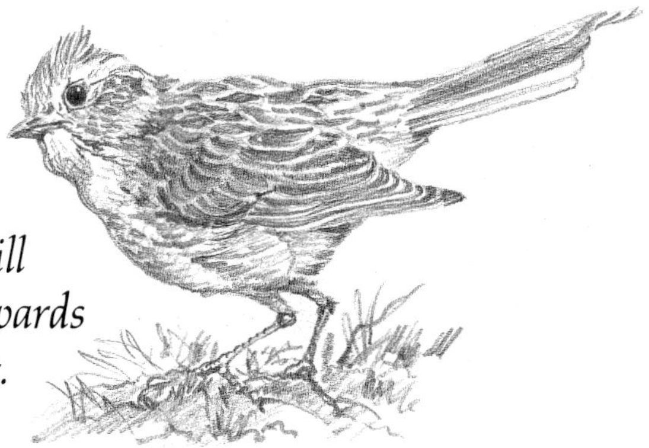

From the crest of the last hill
The land falls away abruptly southwards
To the Channel some three miles distant.
This sudden revelation of sea and sky
Is instinctively uplifting and impels one to cry out,
Like Xenophon's troops in retreat,
"Thalassa! Thalassa!", the sea! the sea!
This is the skylark's view,
Can you wonder his song is one of exaltation?

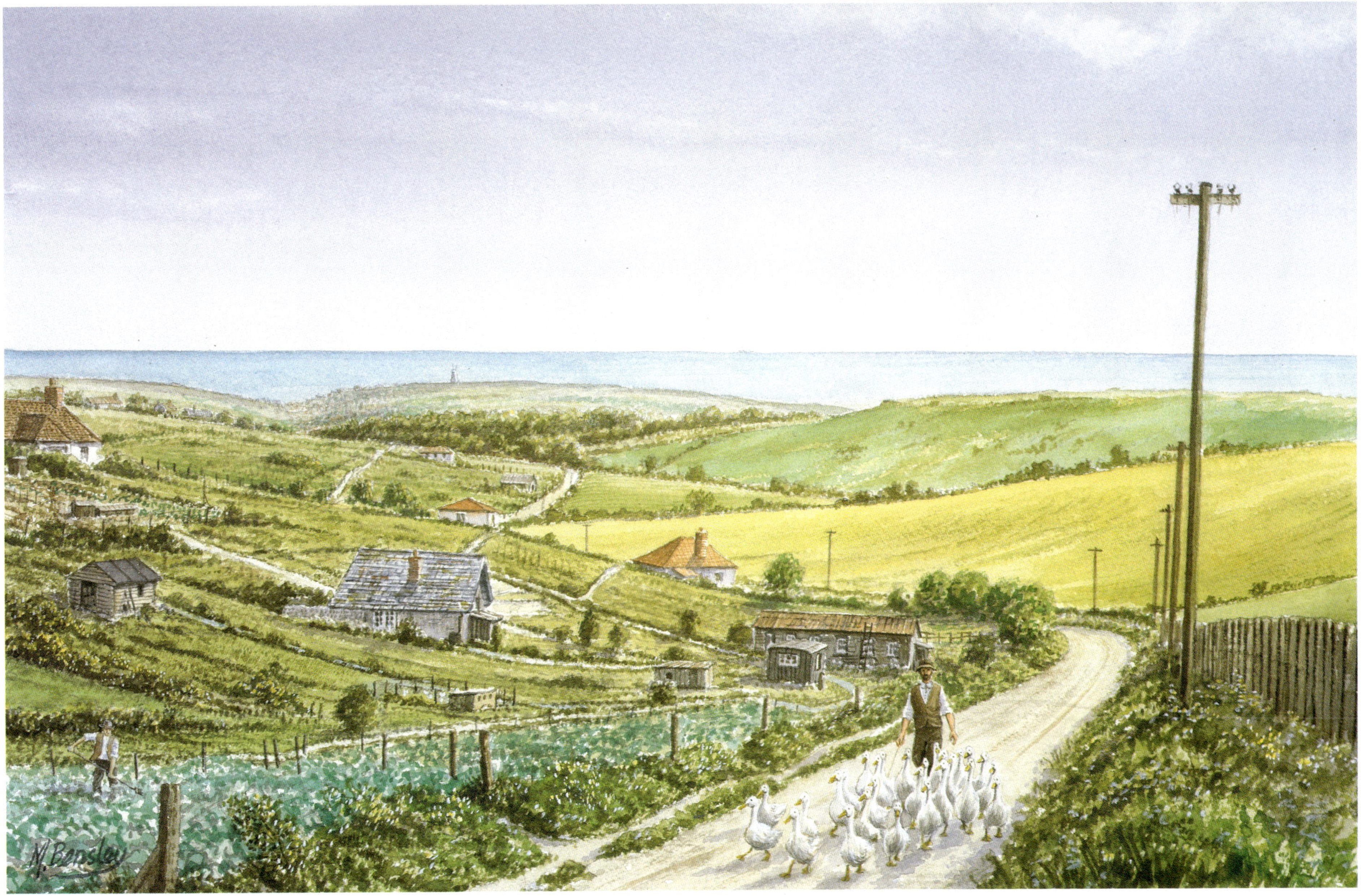
M. Bensley

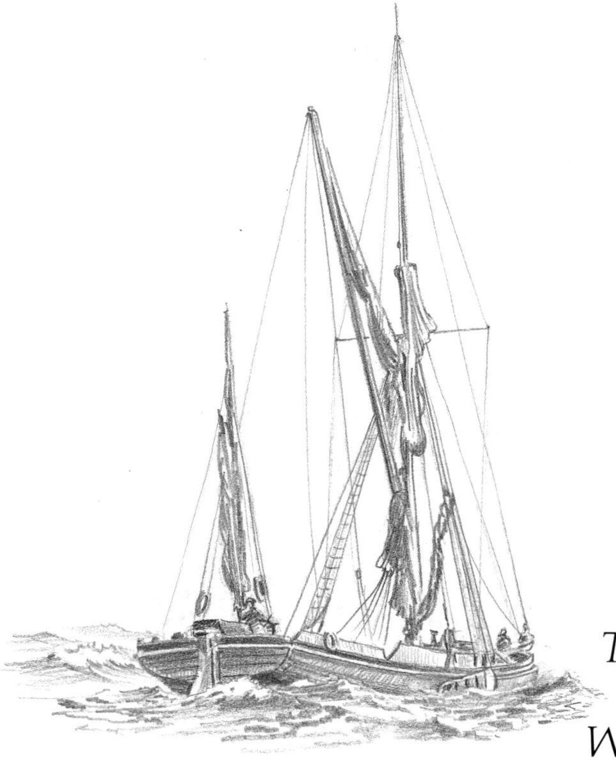

Boomie Barge leaving Newhaven
Watercolour 10 x 16 ins 1998

These sturdy little coasters that sailed south-eastern waters
Like nautical work-horses before the days of steam,
Were built to face the onslaughts of a stormy North Sea winter
And were fitted out with lee-boards and built generous in the beam.

Calling in at any seaport and nosing up the rivers
They had many different cargoes battened down inside the hold:
There was china-clay from Cornwall, building bricks from Belgium,
And Black Forest timber balks and Tyneside coal.

(With a nod and a wink at John Masefield.)

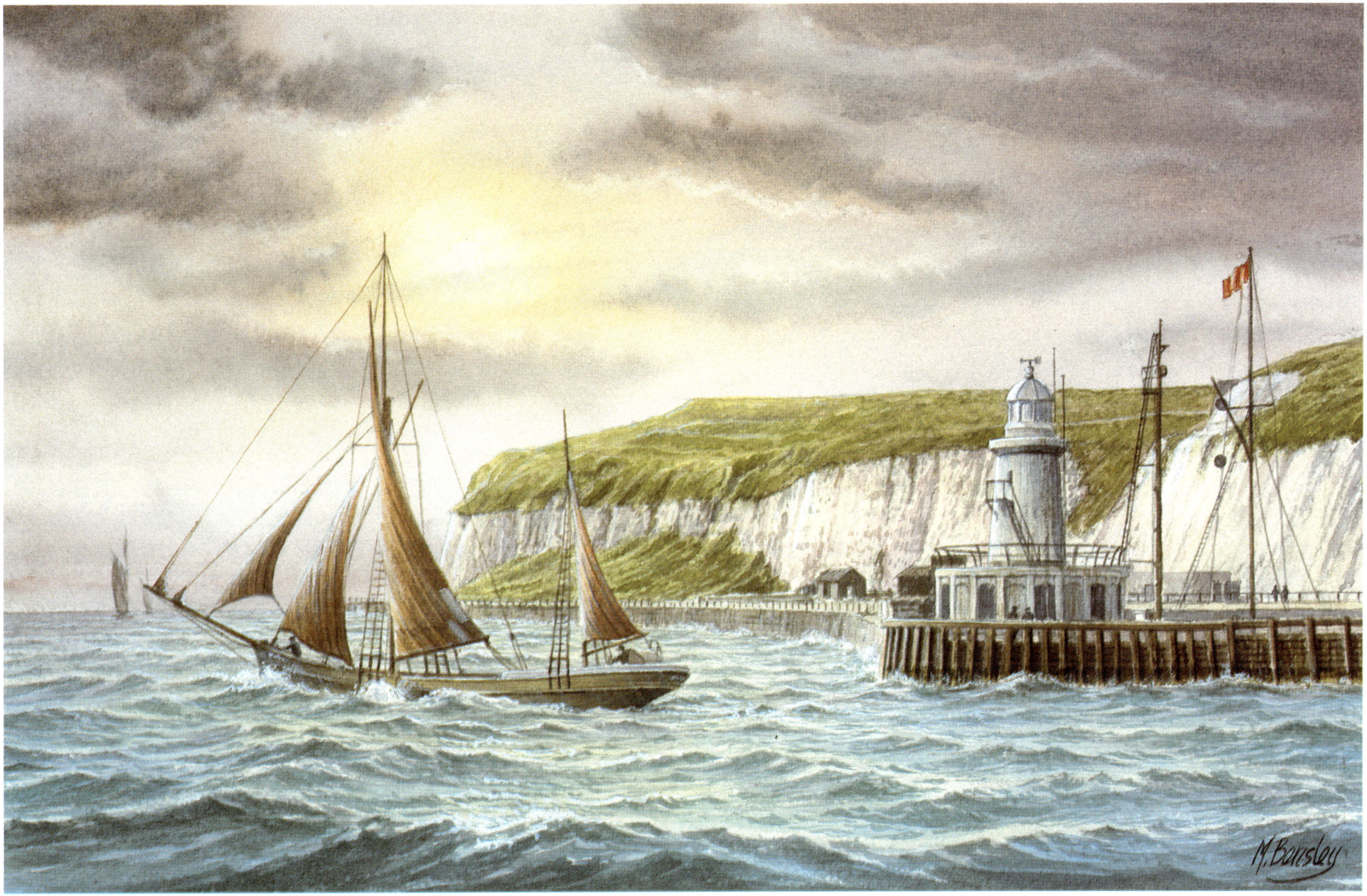
M. Bowsley

Alfriston, the Dray unloading
Watercolour 10 x 16 ins 1997

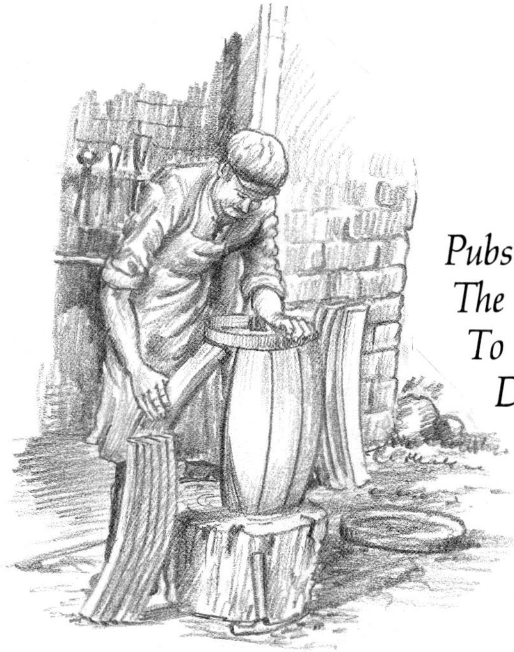

Pubs at the roadside and bars in the street,
The brewer's dray visits wherever folk meet.
To taverns and beer-houses, venerable inns,
Delivering kilderkins, firkins and pins.
Whether nut-brown or amber the liquor they bring
Will deaden a sorrow or make a man sing,
Will lighten his load or make easy his task
If in moderation he sups from the cask.

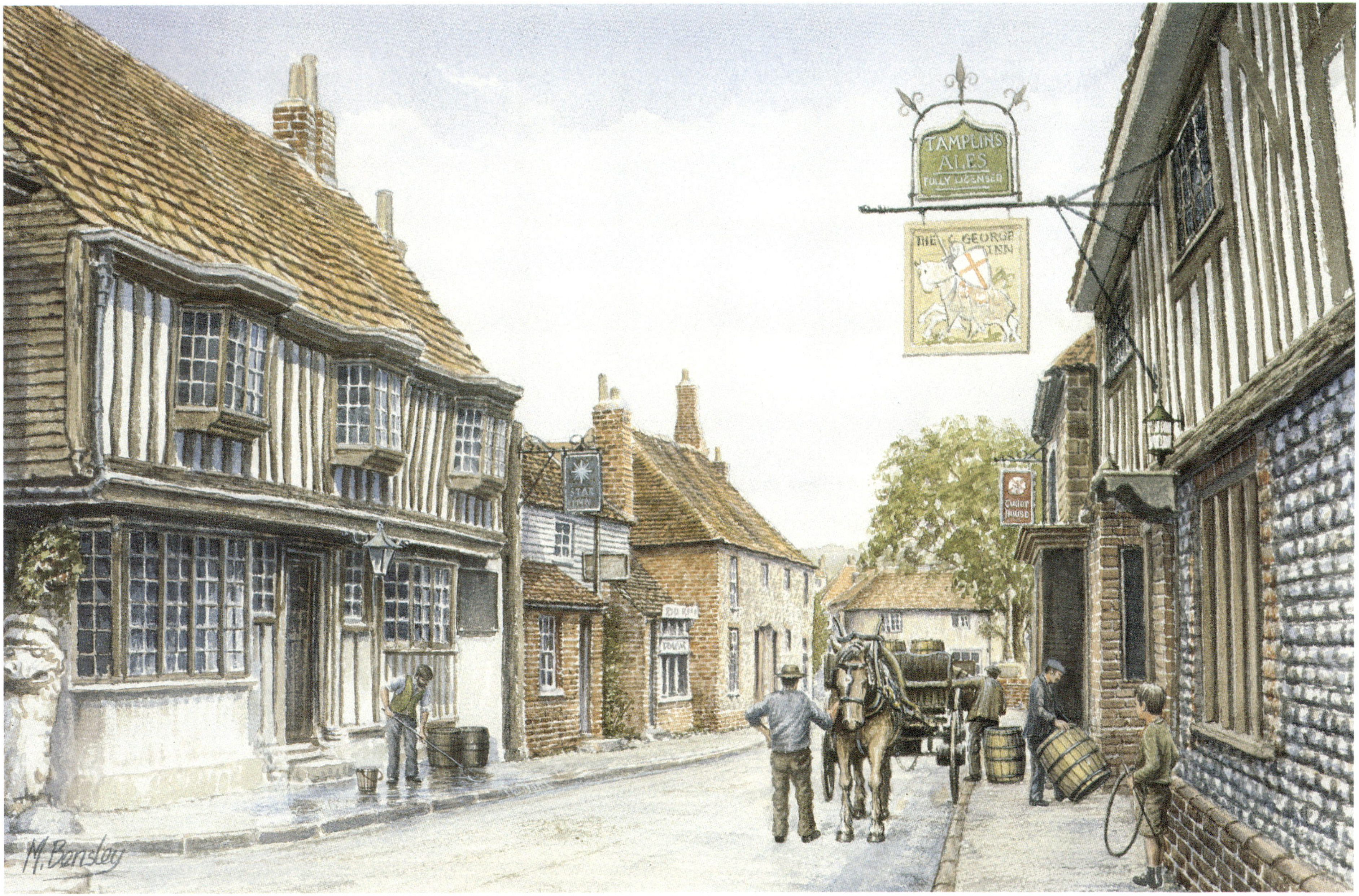
TAMPLINS
ALES
FULLY LICENSED
THE GEORGE INN
STAR INN
Tudor house
M. Bensley

The Gap, Rottingdean
Watercolour 13 x 20 ins 1998

*To the south of the village the street terminated
In a rough, flinty track that led down to the shore
Through a gap in the cliffs, where the local longshore-men
Had cabins wherein their sea-tackle was stored.*

*These fishermen's huts, leaning one on the other,
Smelt of old bloater-boxes and pipes of black shag,
And were stuffed full of anchors and bait-tins and rowlocks,
And cork-lines and seine-nets and fish-scaly rags.*

*And varied and rare were the sights they had witnessed
From smugglers at night running in contraband,
To men carting catches of lobsters or herring;
Or sometimes a group of grim beach-combers bearing
A sad, crumpled body washed up on the sand.*

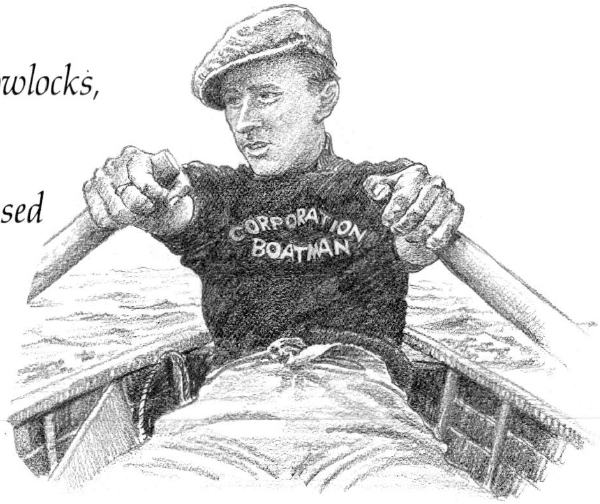

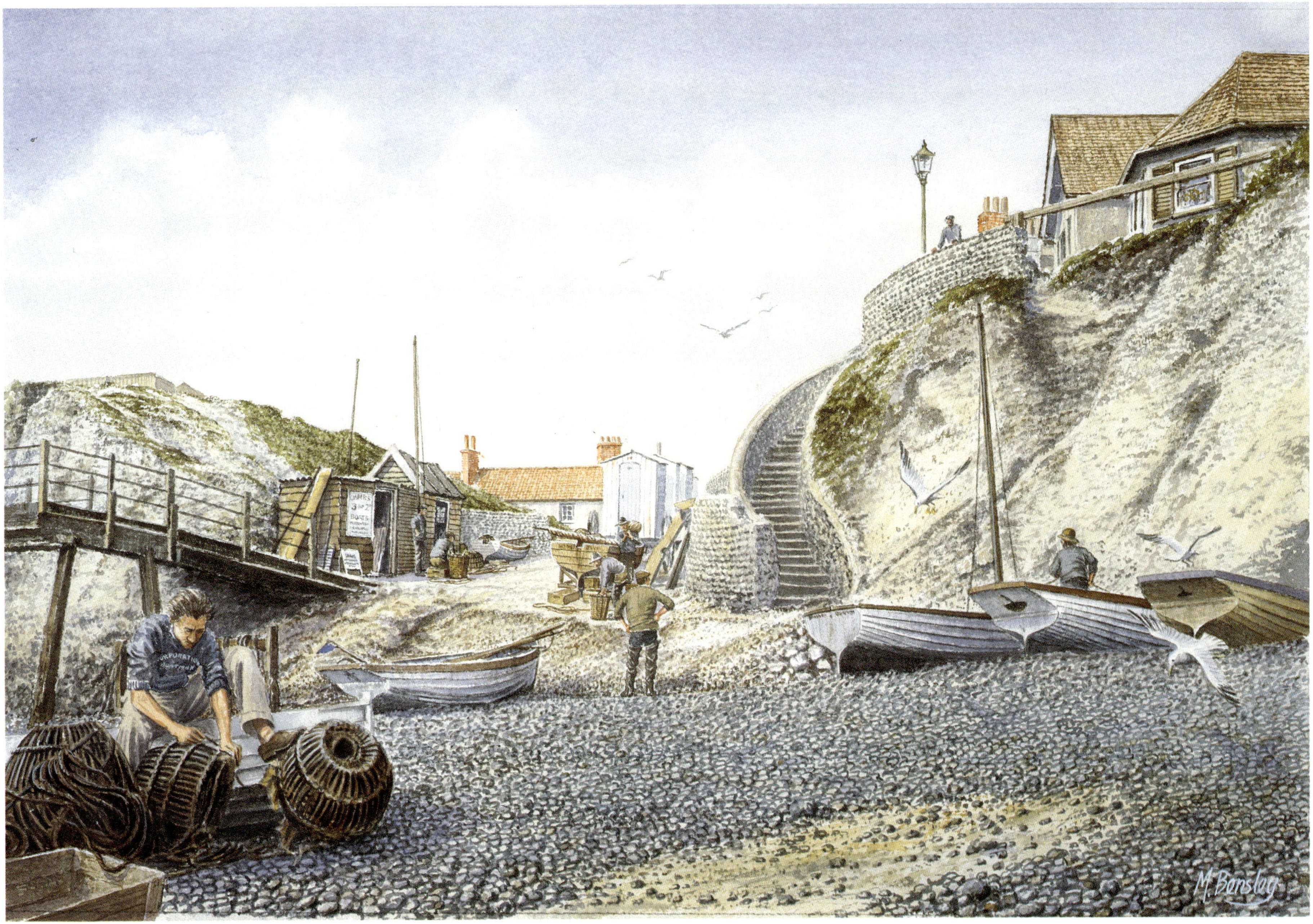
M. Bensley

Southease Barn

Watercolour 10 x 16 ins 1998

Come, all you trusty ploughmen
Of courage bright and bold,
Who labour all the winter
In the stormy wind and cold
To clothe our fields with plenty,
Our farmyards to renew;
That bread may not be wanting
Behold the painful plough.

. . But were it not for ploughmen
Both rich and poor would rue,
For we are all dependent
Upon the faithful plough.

Old Song

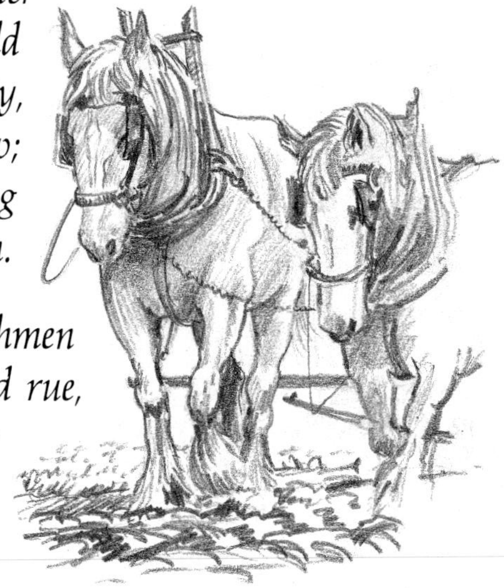

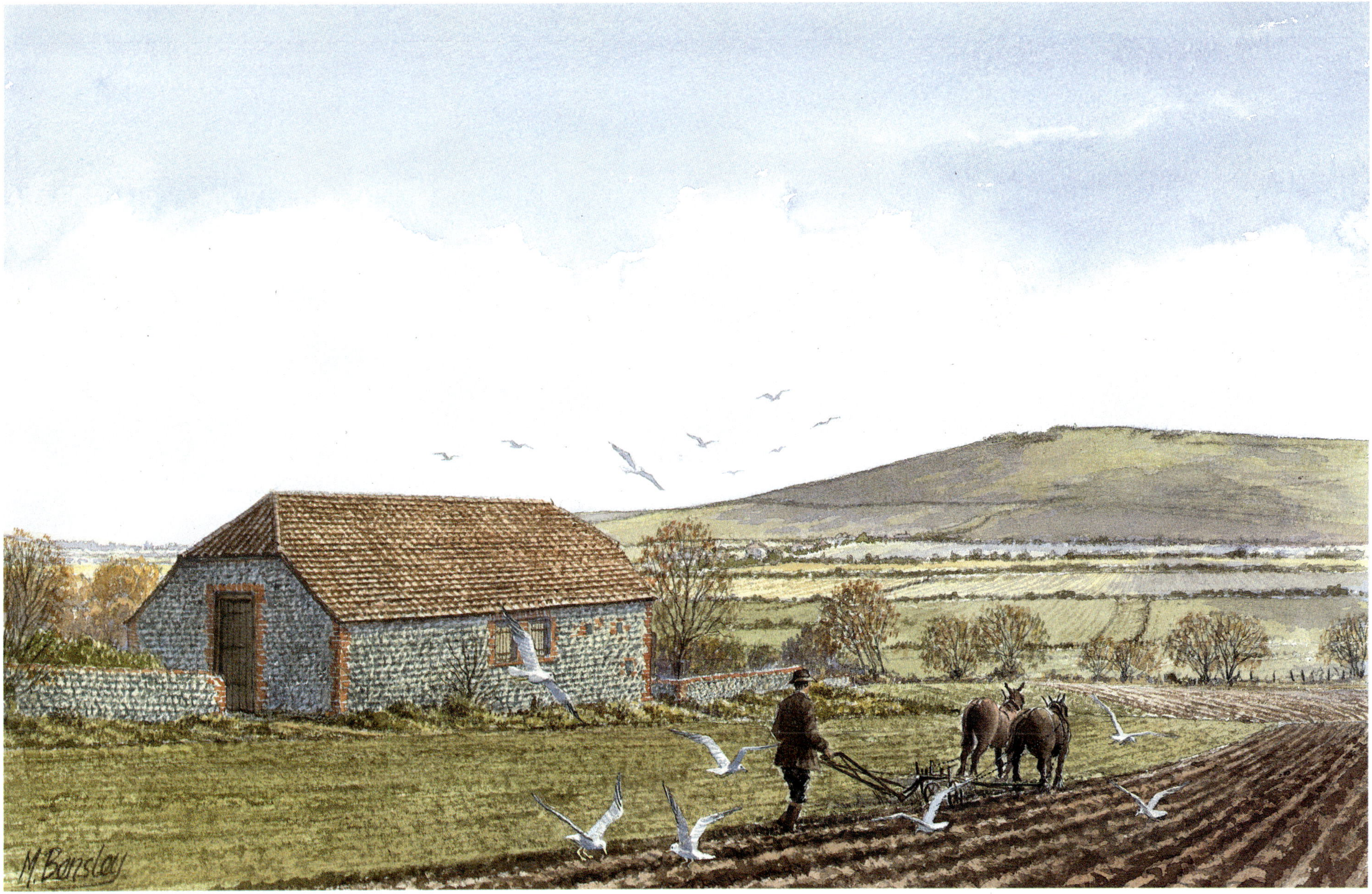
M. Bansley

The Newhaven lifeboat 'Michael Henry' on call to
the 'Emma Louisa' in thick fog off Beachy Head, May 1904
Watercolour 9 x 12 ins 1995

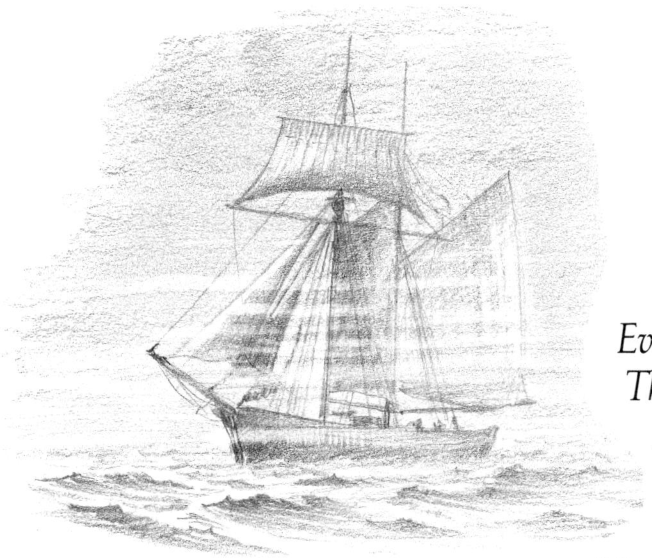

Even when the day was calm with
The waters in a pacific mood and deceptively benign,
A skipper would not dare drop his guard;
For without the slightest warning sign,
And was his fate ill-starred,
He could run into a smothering blanket of fog
Which closely wrapped him round,
And robbed him of all vision.
Then like a blindman with neither stick nor dog
He would drift off course and maybe run aground.

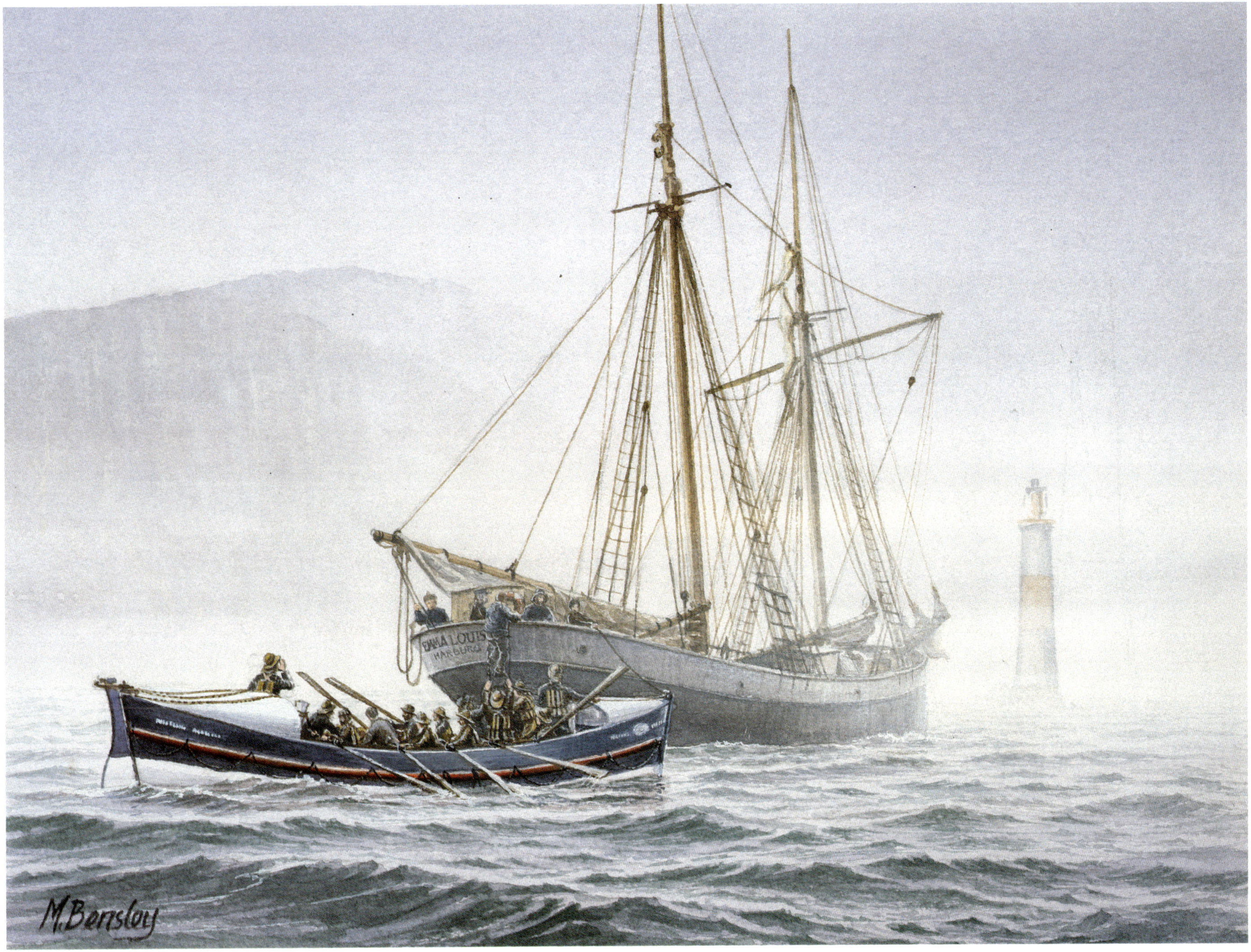
M.Bensley

Ditchling Crossroads

Watercolour 9½ x 15 ins 1997

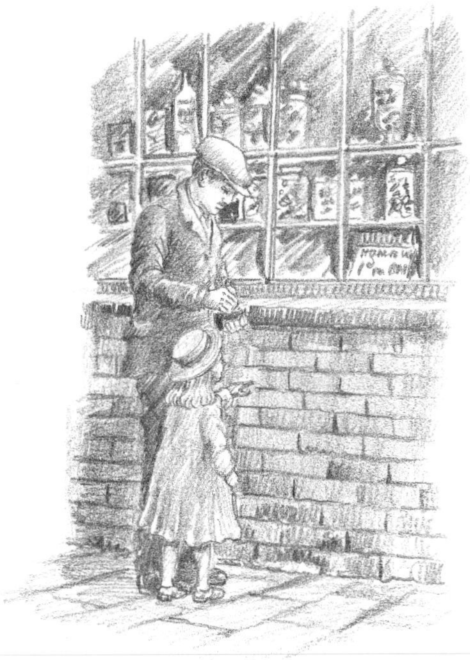

When power from men and horses came
And life was paced more leisurely,
The great world circled just the same
But gave more time for you and me
To meet and greet, and nod and smile,
To talk and laugh and pass the while.

We took the moments as they came,
With time to watch the cornfields grow,
To get to know our fellow-men,
E'en time, perhaps, ourselves to know.

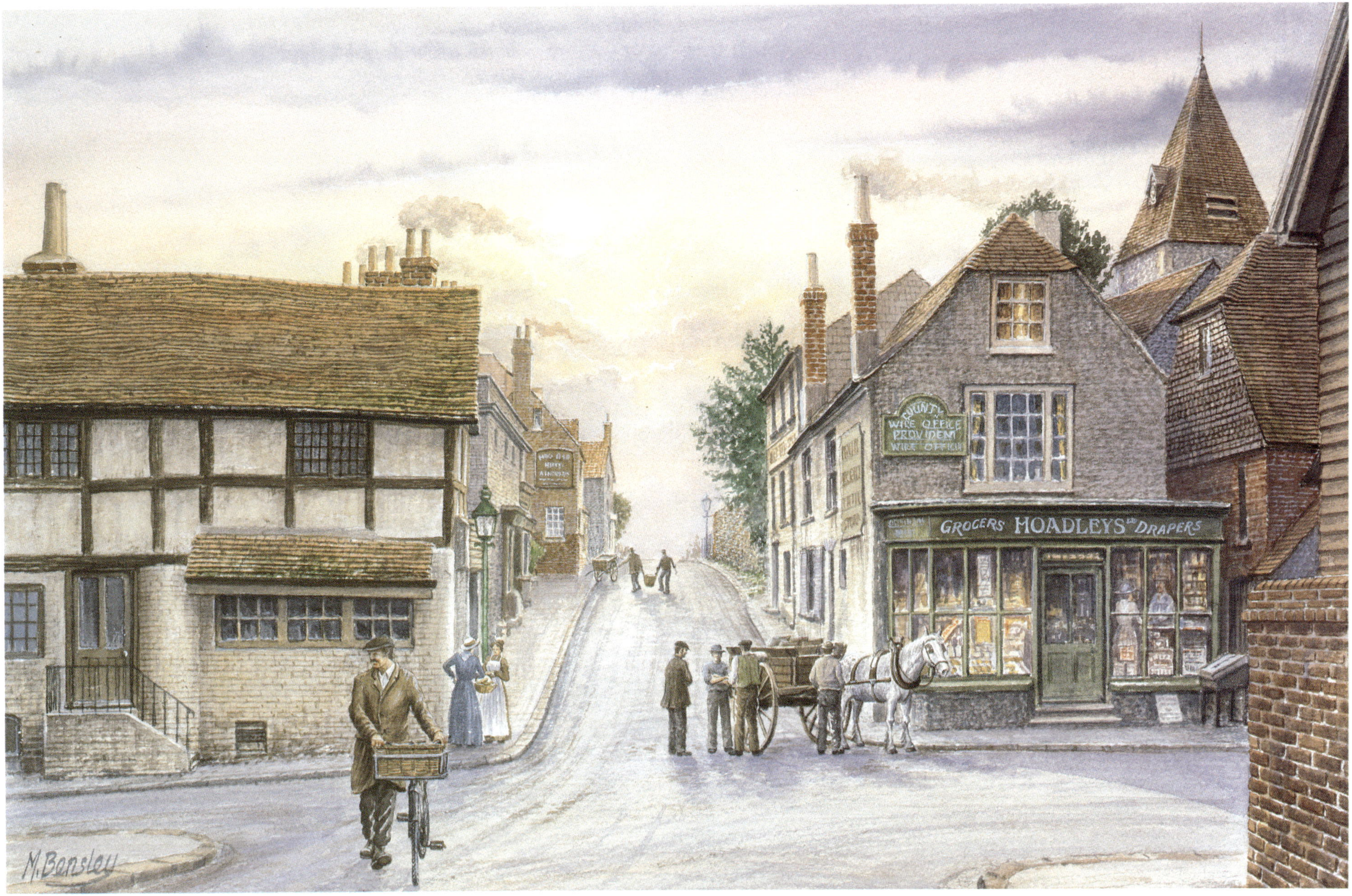
GROCERS HOADLEYS DRAPERS
PROVIDENT
M.Bensley

Newlands Farm, Saltdean

Watercolour 11½ x 18 ins 1998

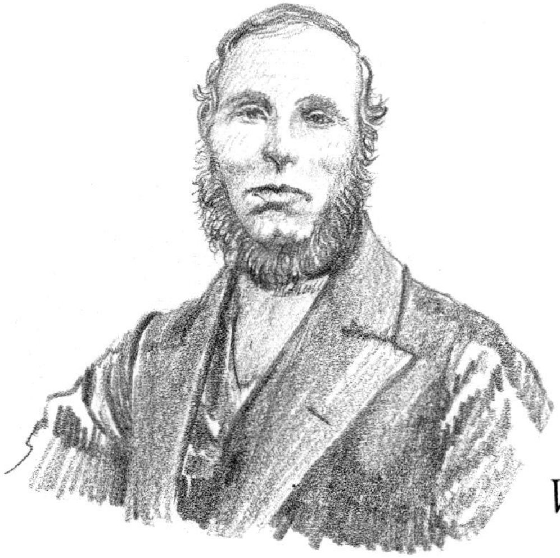

In an isolated cottage in the valley of Saltdean,
When smuggling was still rampant in eighteen seventeen,
My double-great grandfather had a strong and lusty son
Who lived to be respected by the name of Honest John.

And many a time in bed at night he'd hear a splashing oar
And see the lanterns bobbing as they ran their goods ashore.
He'd hear hoof-beats retreating as their horses trotted by,
But he'd sink back into sleep and turn the custom'ry "blind eye".

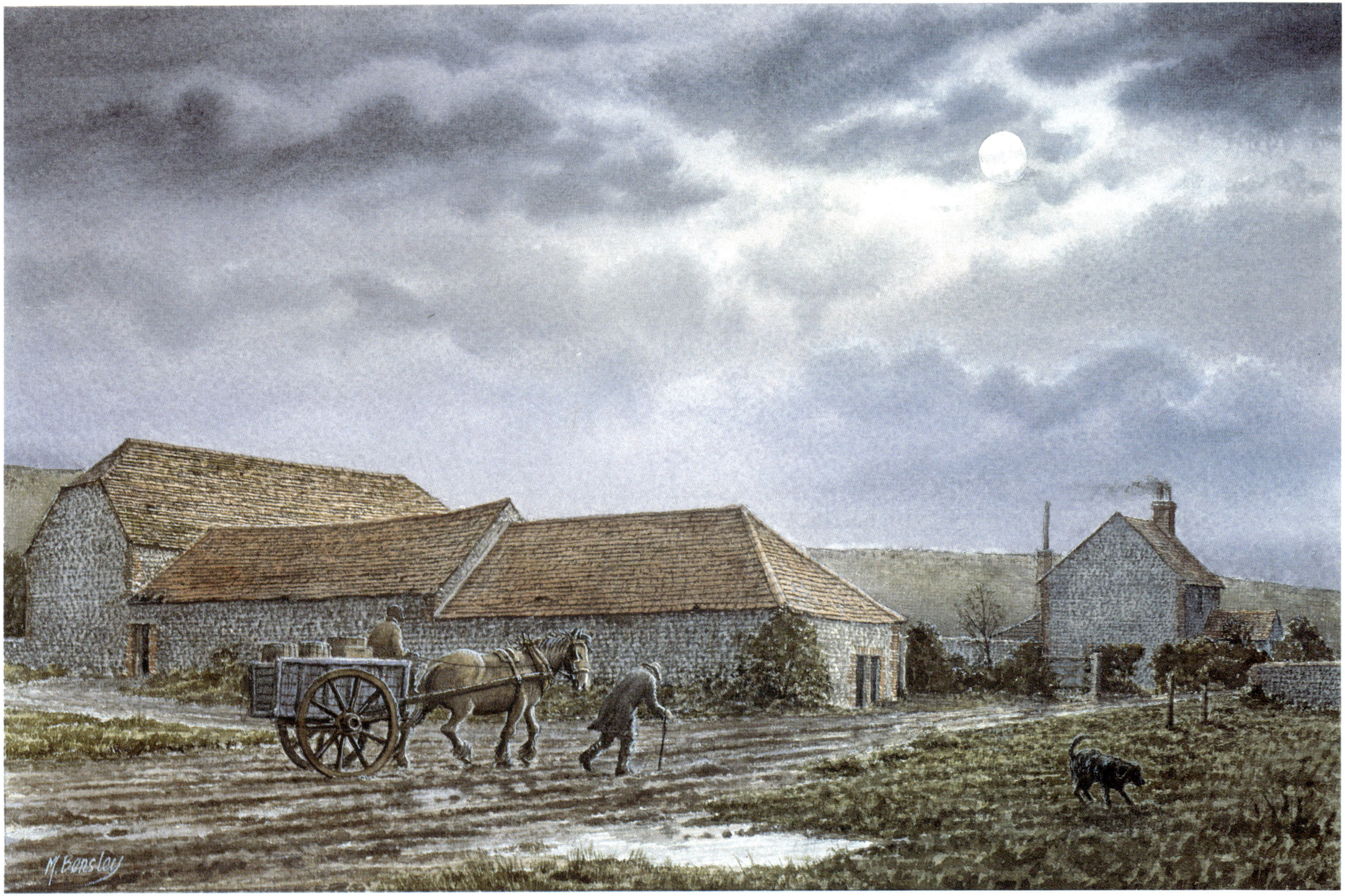
M. Bensley

Haymaking, Rottingdean
Watercolour 10 x 16 ins 1998

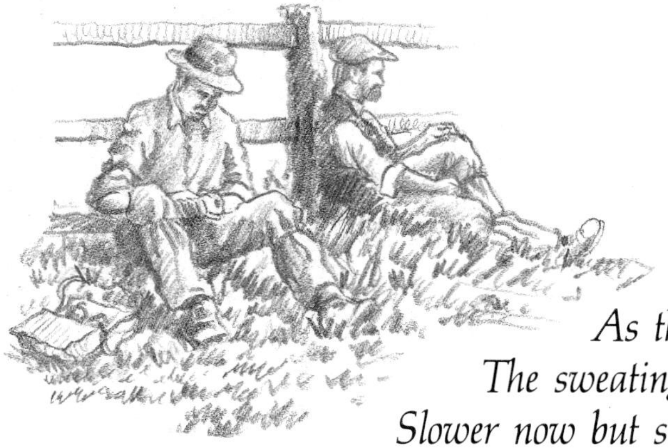

Late on into the summer evening
As the light glows golden and the shadows grow long,
The sweating labourers move their weary limbs
Slower now but steady still and strong.

While from the church the heartening sound of the organ
And choir-voices rehearsing Sunday's hymns.

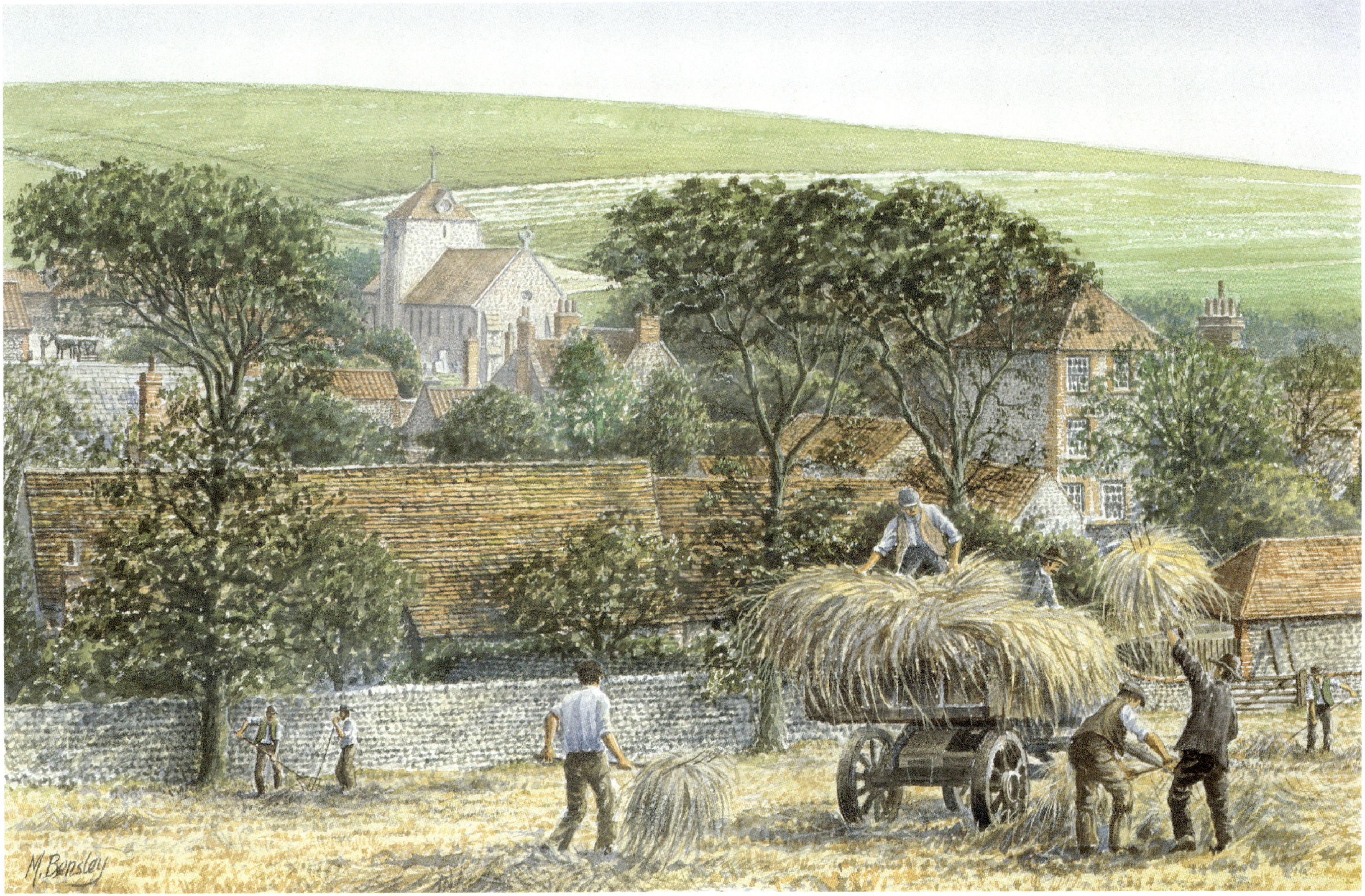
M. Bensley

Leaving Littlehampton

Watercolour 9 x 15 ins 1997

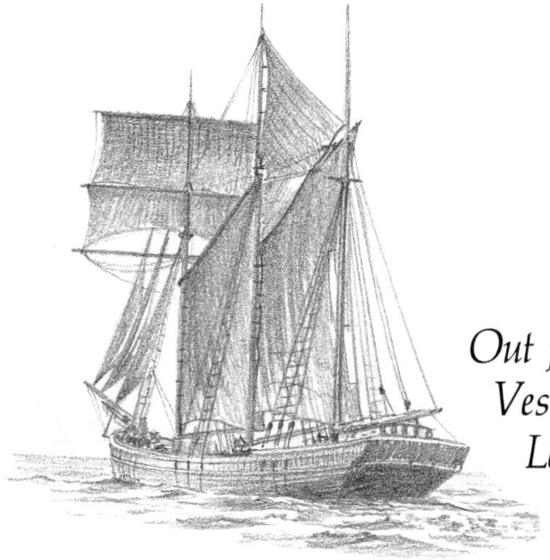

Out from a Sussex harbour a tug-assisted
Vessel heads for the open sea,
Leaving its home port for sunnier climes
Where grows the ban-yan tree.
Where skies are blue and the sun will
Blister the caulking in the seams
And dusky maidens flaunt their charms.
But the Sussex crew will cherish dreams
Of bliss within their sweethearts' arms,
Where Arun winds between the water-meadows,
And ruminating cows stand knee-deep in green pastures.

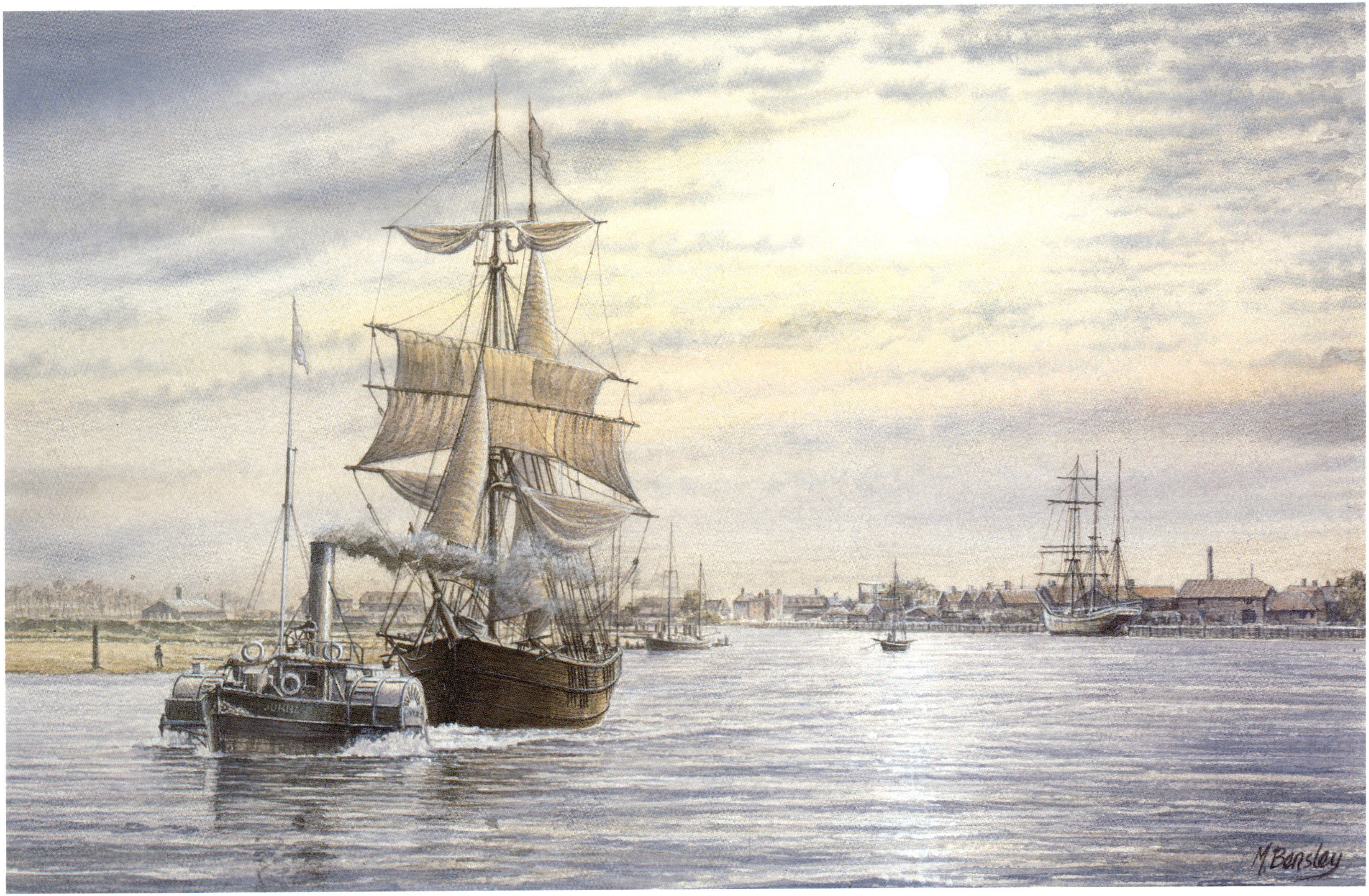
M. Bensley

The Smithy, Bolney

Watercolour 10 x 16 ins 1997

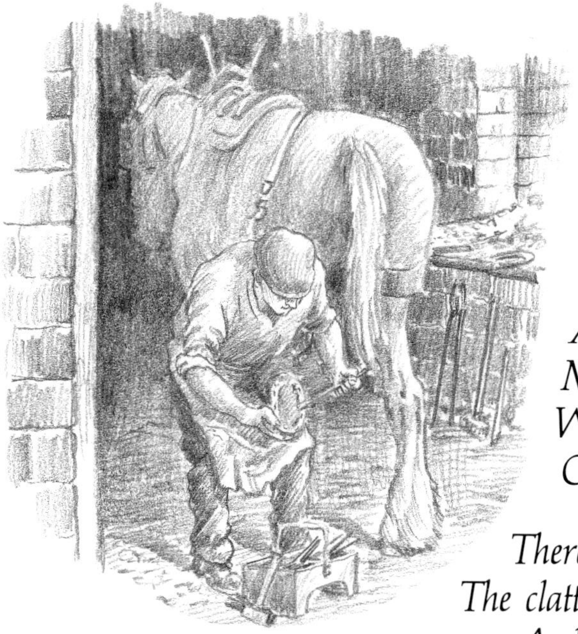

An autumn day and peace is all around.
Men go steadily about their jobs
Without fuss, quietly
Contributing to the common weal.

There is no sound save the tapping of a hammer;
The clatter of pincers dropped to the ground,
And a dog barking three fields away.
The damp, mellow scents of October
Are laced with the sharp, acrid stench
Of singeing hoof.

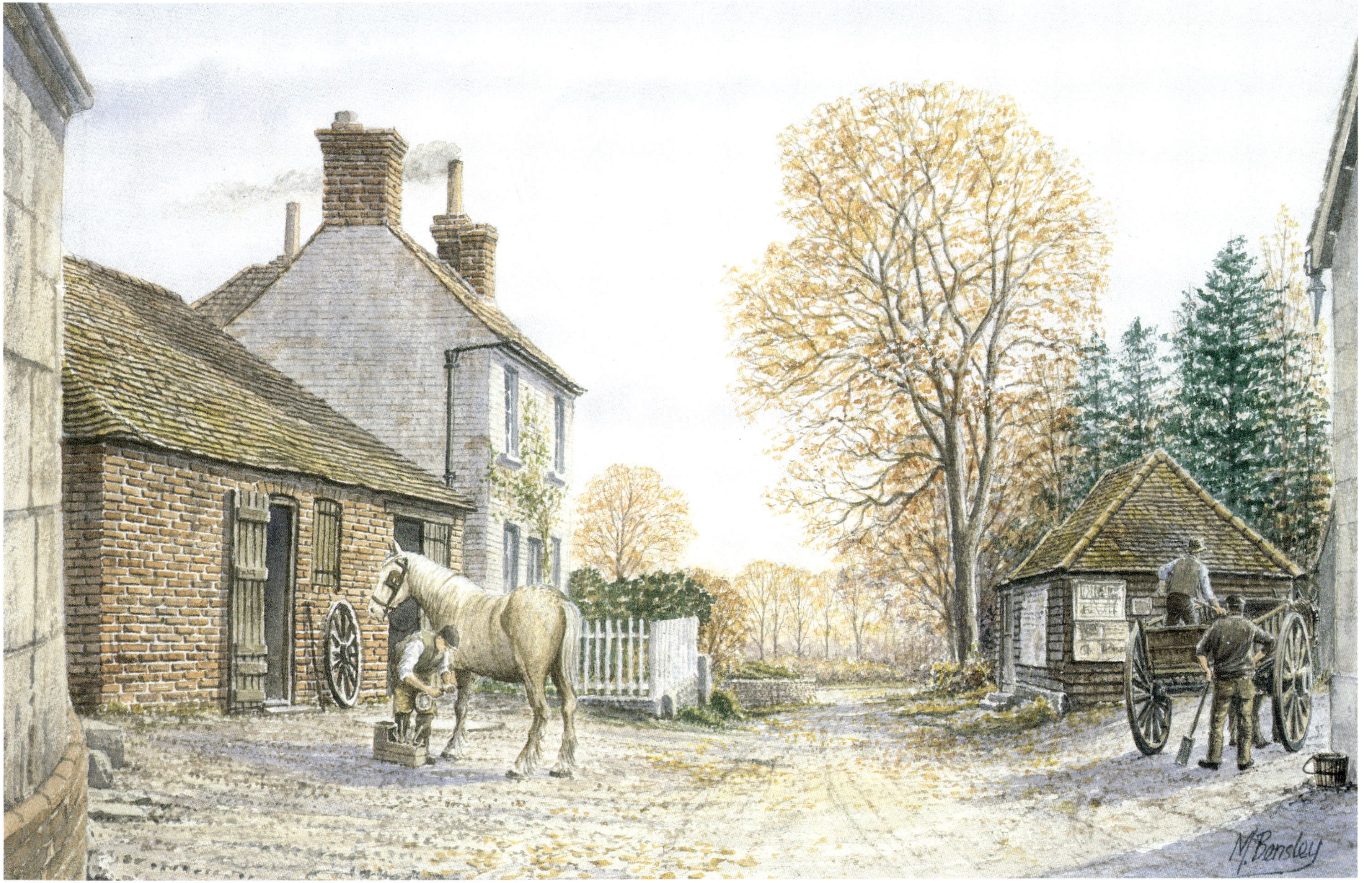
M. Bensley

December morning, Rottingdean
Watercolour 10 x 16 ins 1998

Winter's white and snowy mantle,
Falling softly in the night,
Bestows a dignity revealed
Of a venerable lady with shawl of purest white
Draped about her shoulders:
Workaday blemishes and the ravages
Of Time alike concealed.

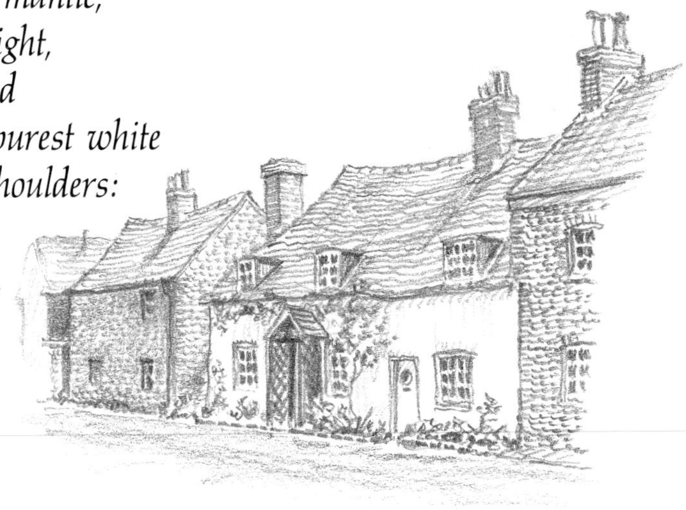

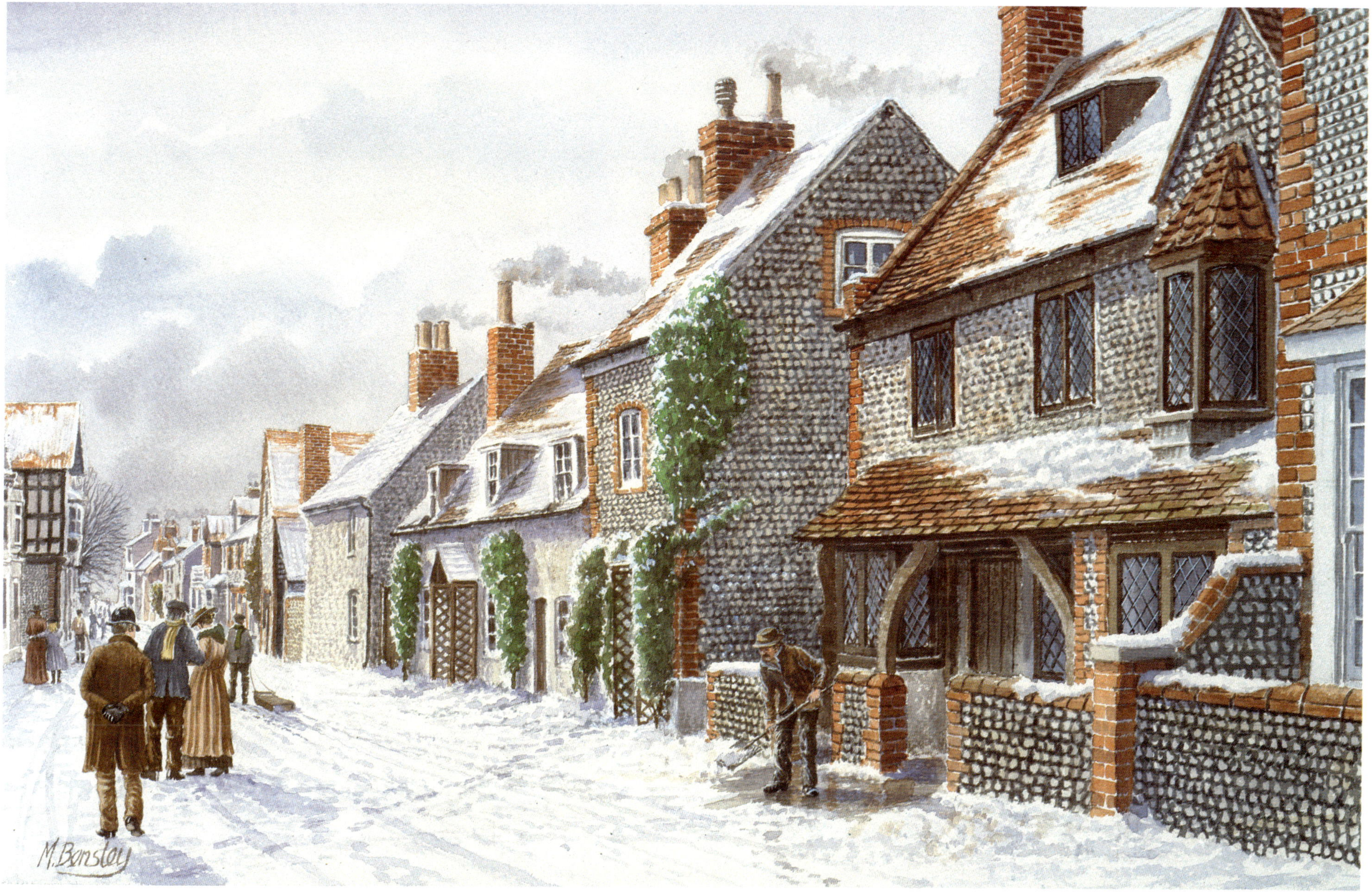

The Volk's Railway at Rottingdean Pier

Watercolour 10 x 16 ins 1997

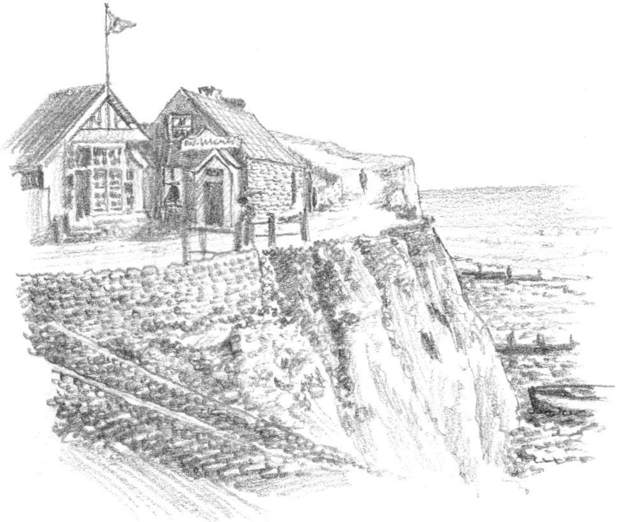

Amazed at technology's latest appliance
Bank-holiday visitors cause quite a stir,
In scrambling to take full advantage of science
And go for a sea-trip without mal de mer.

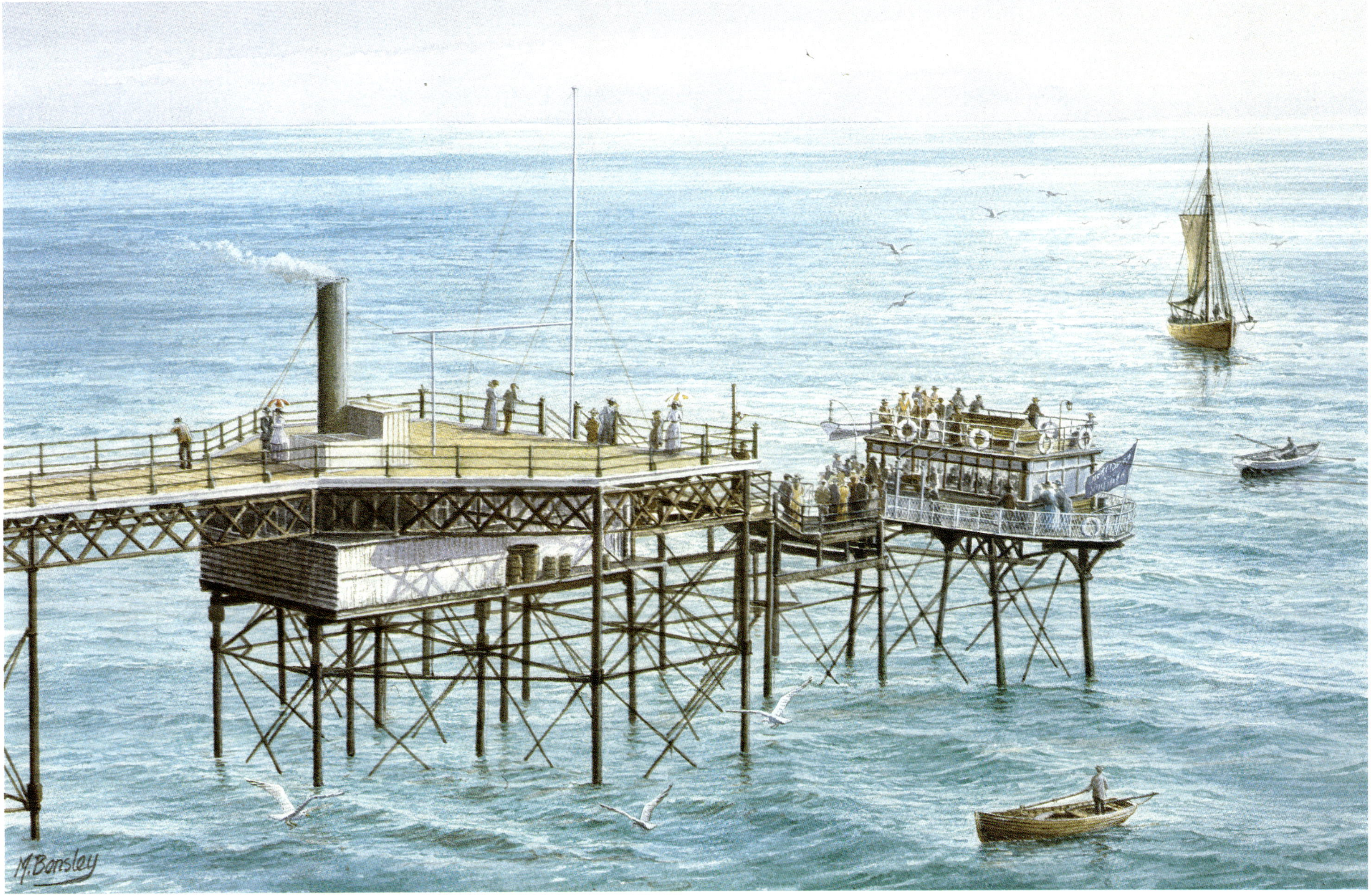
M.Bonsley

Barge unloading at Bury

Watercolour 10 x 16 ins 1997

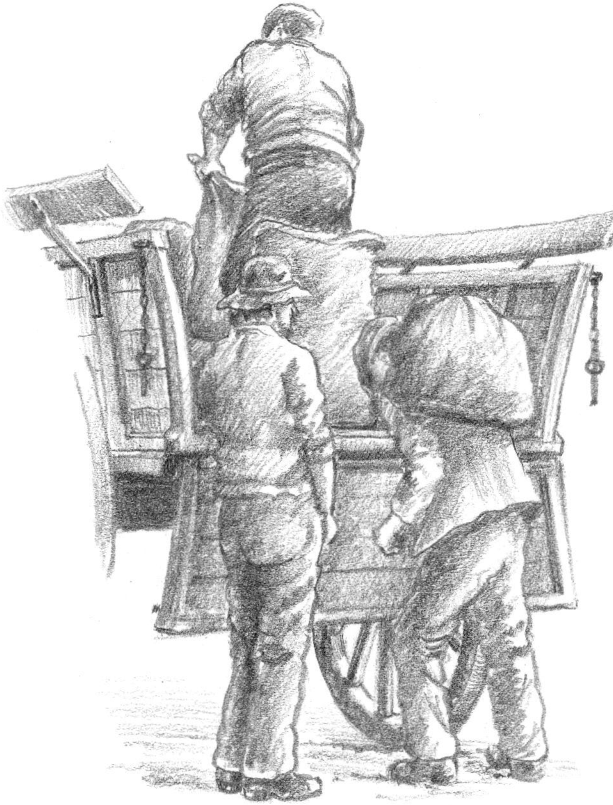

*A barge's arrival signals a flutter
Of unaccustomed activity.
Wagons rumble down to the wharf,
Men roll their sleeves and brace their backs,
Shout at the horses, joke and laugh,
As a prelude to strenuous action.
Then one by one the swollen sacks
Are brought on land.*

*At last the barge departs,
The wagons withdraw and the peace of Bury
Surges softly back again to embrace
The church, the farm and the idle ferry.*

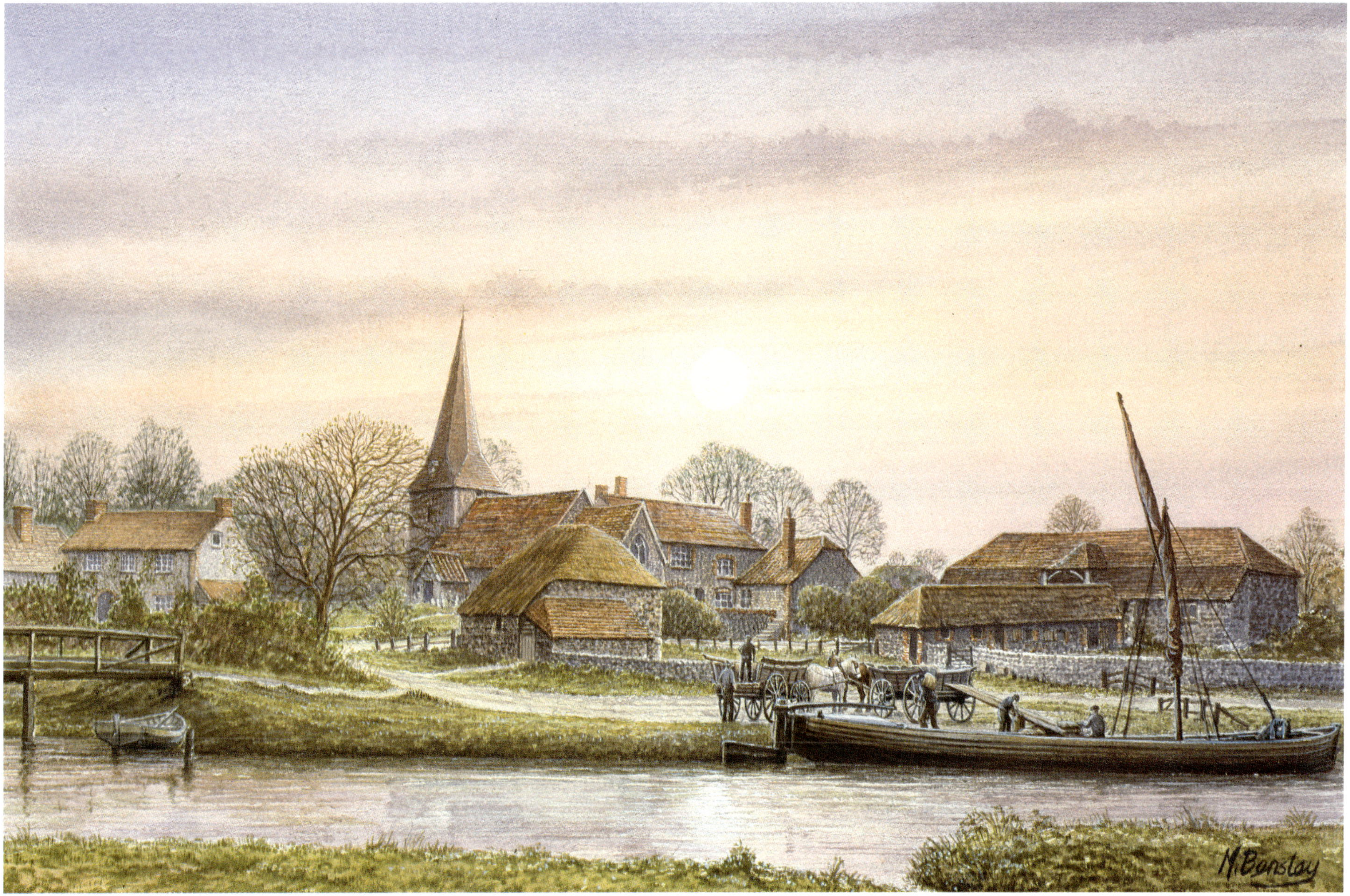
M. Bensley

The Newhaven lifeboat 'Sir Fitzroy Clayton' on call
to the brigantine 'Catherine', March 1914
Watercolour 10 x 13 ins 1994

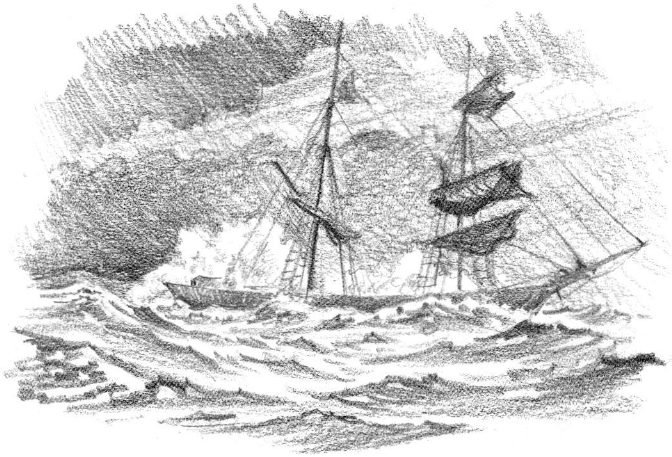

Out from the boatyard, the coal-wharf or stable
In haste that will brook neither check nor delay,
They rally their courage, both willing and able
To answer the call, "There's a ship in the Bay".

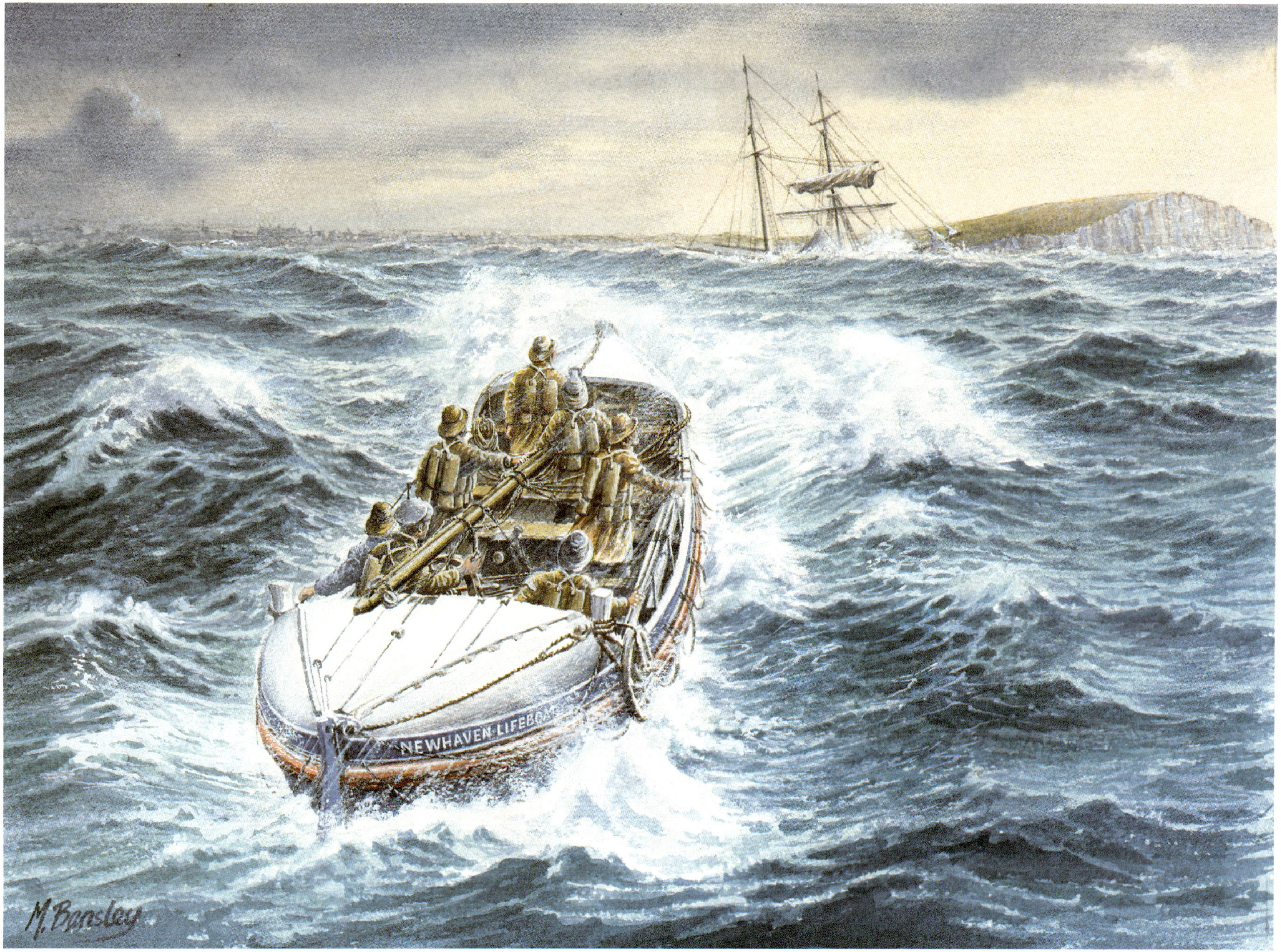
NEWHAVEN LIFEBOA
M. Bensley

Hastings, sorting the catch

Watercolour 12 x 20 ins 1993

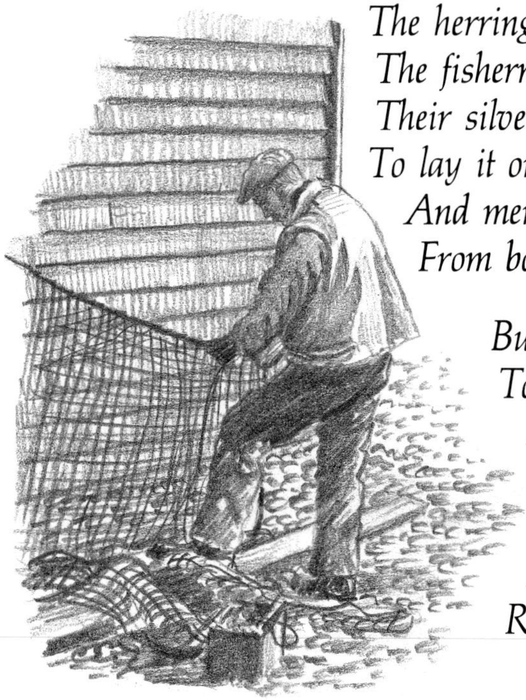

With the golden harvest of the land
Safely housed in barn and granary,
The herring season was at hand.
The fishermen would cast their nets and haul
Their silver harvest from the sea
To lay it on the strand;
And men drew succour
From both field and wave.

But that was ere the pitcher
To the well too often went
And the waters ceased to yield.
Nature's bounty, from ill-management,
Was over-indulged and the poor
Man's breakfast became the
Rich man's luxury.

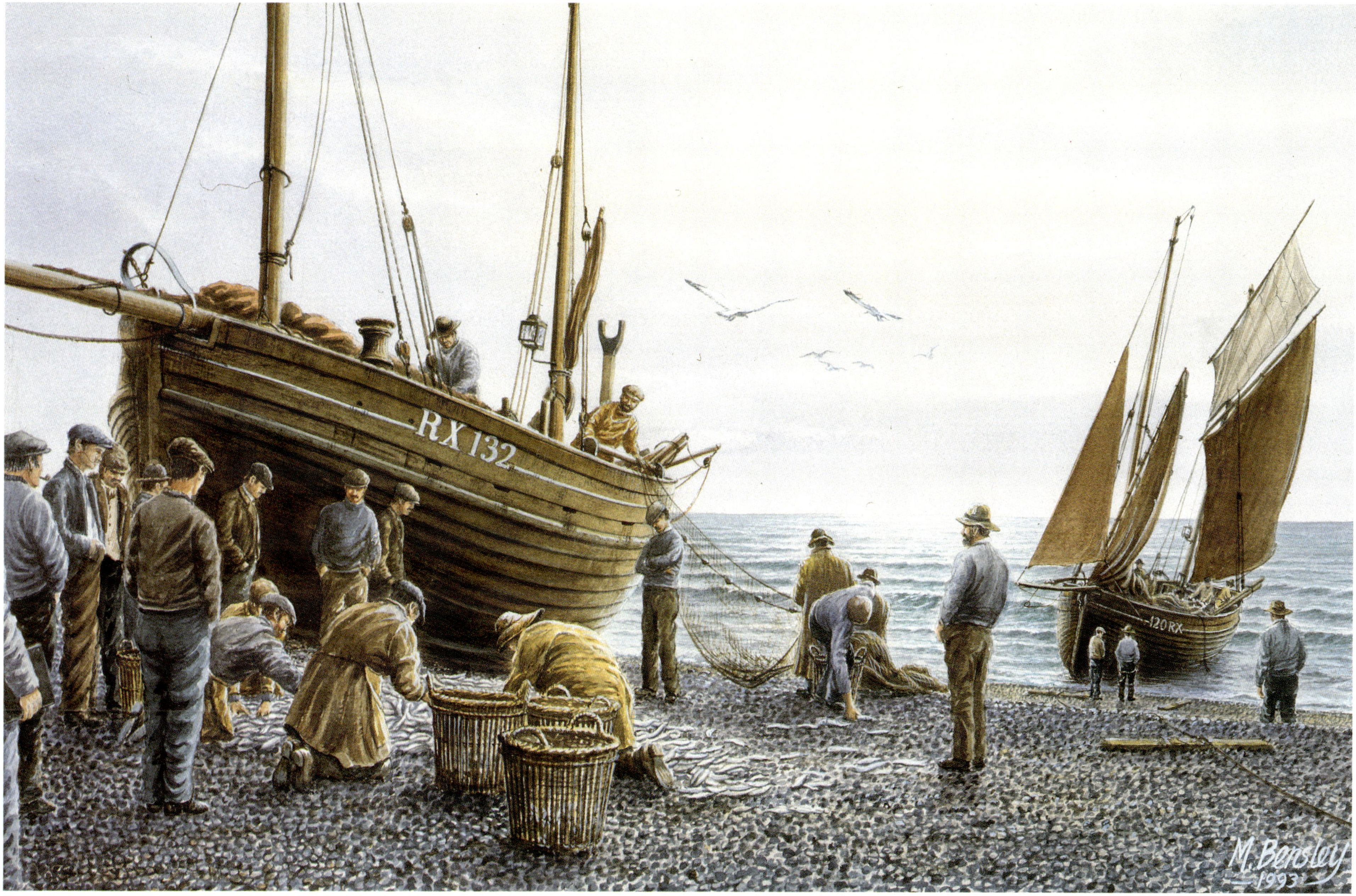
RX 132
120 RX
M. Bensley
1993

Coming ashore

Watercolour 12 x 18¼ ins 1998

When a couple of rowers are coming ashore
There must be between them a perfect understanding
Of plan, and in execution complete co-ordination.
And this is true,
Particularly, when each is handling a single oar,
For an extra stroke from one
Will cause a catastrophic landing.
With the boat lying broadside on to the waves
To the utter consternation,
Not to say humiliation,
Of the crew.

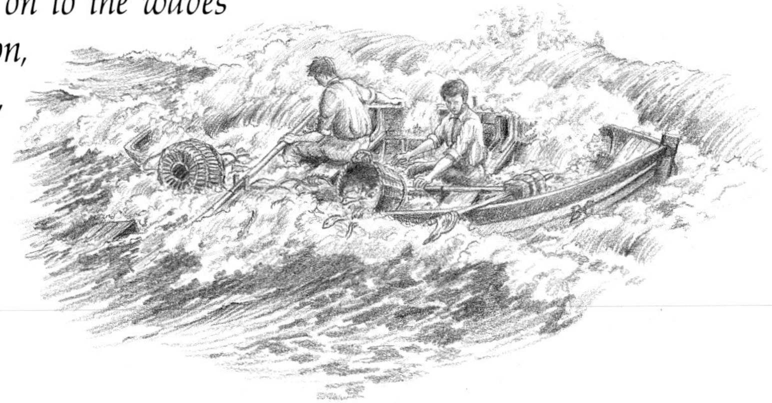

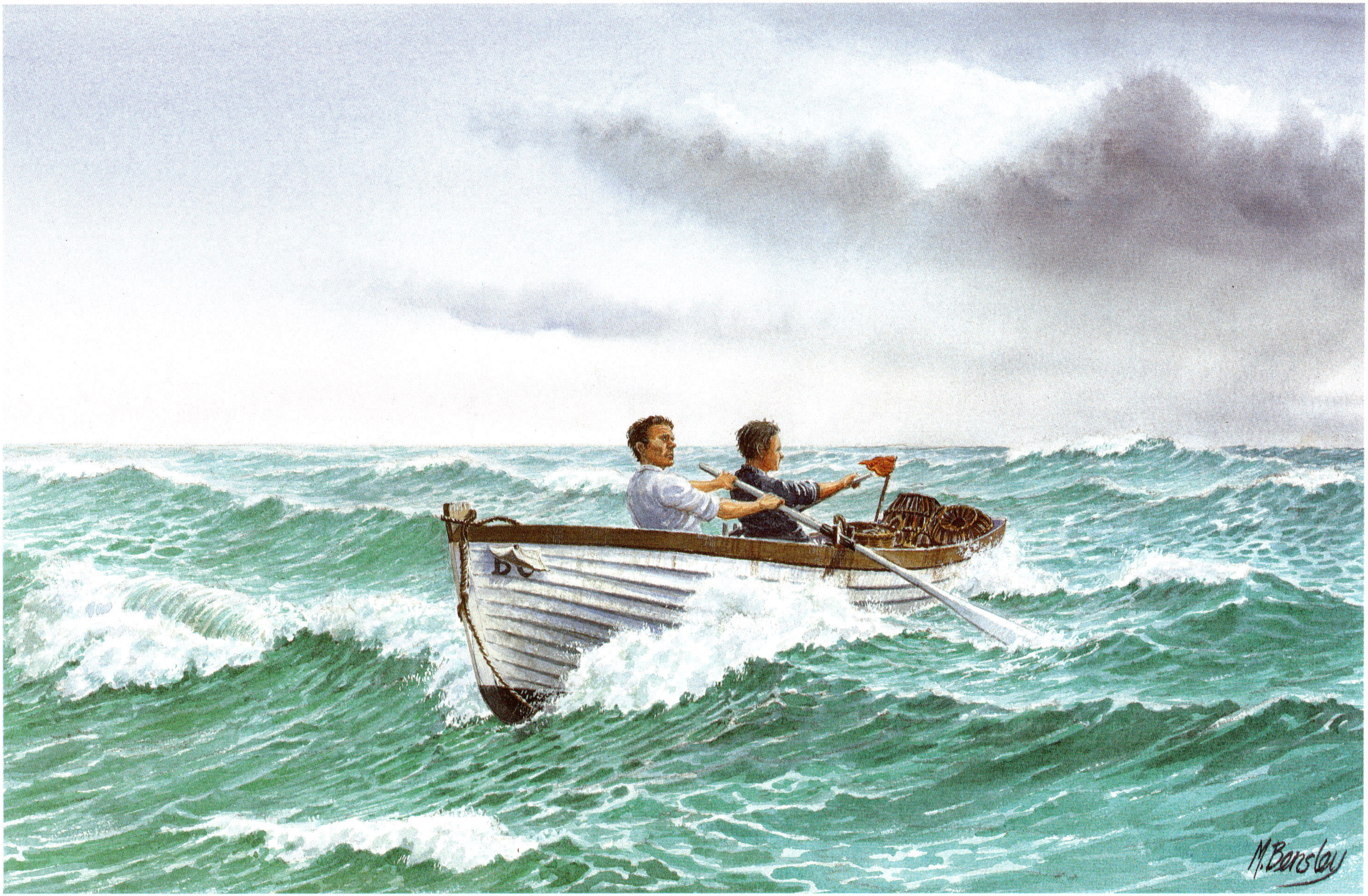

ACKNOWLEDGEMENTS

Thanks are due to the following who have lent paintings for reproduction in this book:

N. Turner
"Rye, Winter Sun"

M. Tubbs
"Newhaven lifeboat on call to the schooner 'Morgens Koch'"

J. & A. Kendall
"Sorting the catch, Hastings"

A. & P. Mallinson
"Fishing boats off Brighton"

The following are in private collections:

"Steyning early start";
"Arundel, February afternoon";
"Shoreham lifeboat on call to the Anirac";
"Alfriston"; "Leaving Littlehampton";
"The Smithy, Bolney";
"Pilgrim rescue off Brighton";
"Barge unloading at Bury";
"Haymaking Rottingdean";
"Newhaven lifeboat on call to the Catherine"
and "Rottingdean Mill".

Thanks also to:

Chromatics (Brighton) for the trannies.
R.N.L.I. for access to their records.
Hartington Fine Arts for the print.
Rottingdean Preservation Society for access to their archives.
And a special thanks to Bob for his verse which perfectly captures the mood of the paintings.

BIBLIOGRAPHY

Blyth, H. *Smugglers Village,* Blyth, 1984.

Copper, B. *Bob Copper's Sussex,* S.B. Publications, 1997.

Copper, B. *A Song for every Season,* Coppersongs, 1997.

Finch, R. *Sailing Craft of the British Isles,* Collins, 1976.

Heater, Derek *The Remarkable History of Rottingdean,* Heater, 1993.

Morris, Jeff and Hendy, Dave *The Story of the Newhaven Lifeboats,* Morris, 1987.

Payne, Tony *Newhaven in old picture postcards — Lifeboats — Wrecks — Rescues,* Payne, 1991.

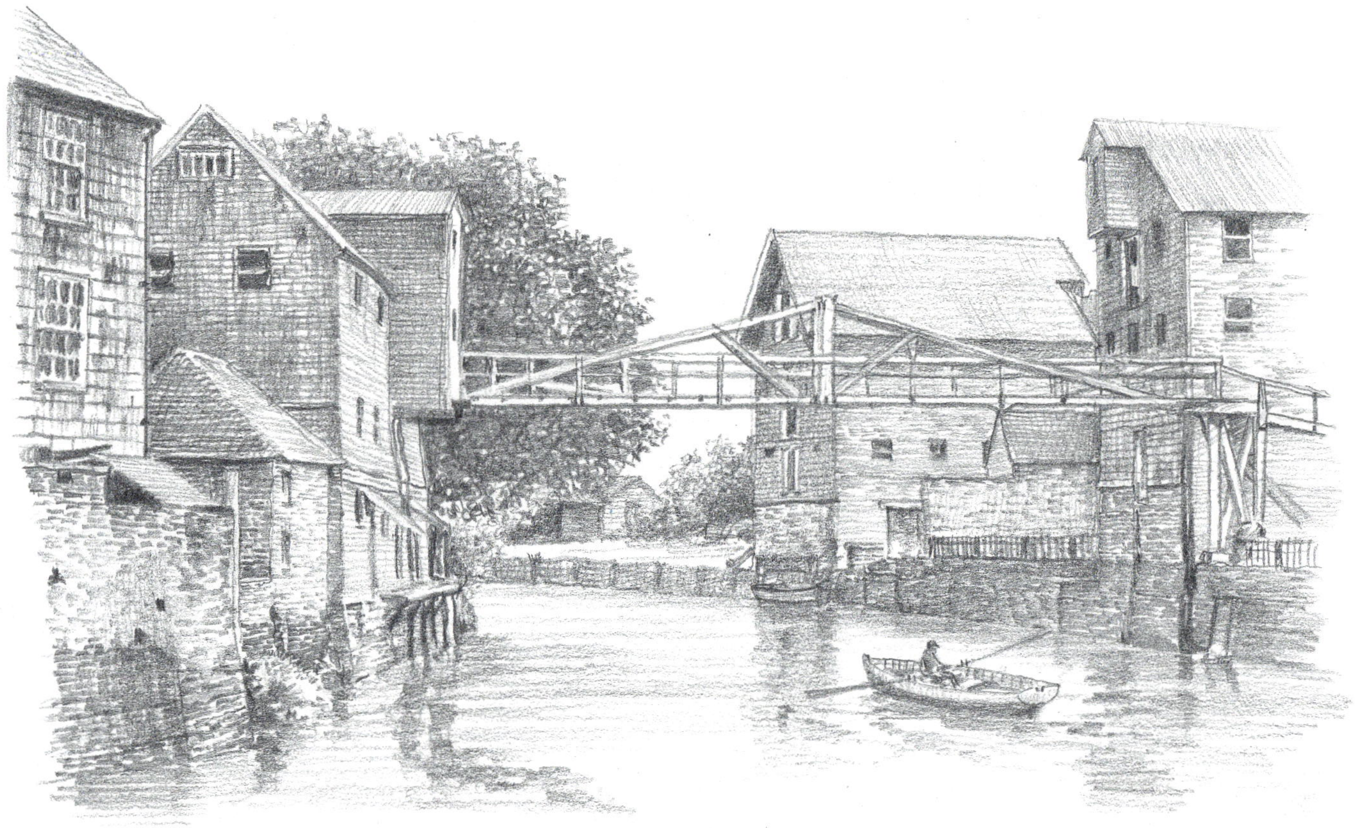